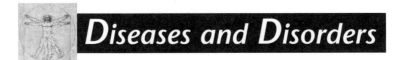

Diseases and Disorders

Food
Poisoning

Titles in the Diseases and Disorders series include:

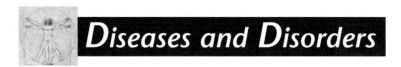
Diseases and Disorders

Food Poisoning

by Barbara Sheen

LUCENT BOOKS
An imprint of Thomson Gale, a part of The Thomson Corporation

Detroit • New York • San Francisco • San Diego • New Haven, Conn. • Waterville, Maine • London • Munich

On cover: A cluster of the bacteria *E. coli,* one of the many pathogens that may cause food poisoning, is pictured in a transmission electron micrograph.

LIBRARY OF CONGRESS CATALOGING-IN-PUBLICATION DATA

Sheen, Barbara.
    Food poisoning / by Barbara Sheen.
        p. cm. — (Diseases and disorders)
Includes bibliographical references and index.
Contents: What is food poisoning?—Diagnosis and treatment—Avoiding food poisoning—Protecting the public—What the future holds.
        ISBN 1-59018-409-2 (hard cover : alk. paper)
1. Food poisoning—Juvenile literature. I. Title. II. Series: Diseases and disorders series
RC143.S445 2004
615.9'54—dc22

                                                                2004011880

Printed in the United States of America

Table of Contents

"The Most Difficult Puzzles Ever Devised"

Charles Best, one of the pioneers in the search for a cure for diabetes, once explained what it is about medical research that intrigued him so. "It's not just the gratification of knowing one is helping people," he confided, "although that probably is a more heroic and selfless motivation. Those feelings may enter in, but truly, what I find best is the feeling of going toe to toe with nature, of trying to solve the most difficult puzzles ever devised. The answers are there somewhere, those keys that will solve the puzzle and make the patient well. But how will those keys be found?"

Since the dawn of civilization, nothing has so puzzled people—and often frightened them, as well—as the onset of illness in a body or mind that had seemed healthy before. A seizure, the inability of a heart to pump, the sudden deterioration of muscle tone in a small child—being unable to reverse such conditions or even to understand why they occur was unspeakably frustrating to healers. Even before there were names for such conditions, even before they were understood at all, each was a reminder of how complex the human body was, and how vulnerable.

While our grappling with understanding diseases has been frustrating at times, it has also provided some of humankind's most heroic accomplishments. Alexander Fleming's accidental discovery in 1928 of a mold that could be turned into penicillin has resulted in the saving of untold millions of lives. The isolation of the enzyme insulin has reversed what was once a death sentence for anyone with diabetes. There have been great strides in combating conditions for which there is not yet a cure, too. Medicines can help AIDS patients live longer, diagnostic tools such as mammography and ultrasounds can help doctors find tumors while they are treatable, and laser surgery techniques have made the most intricate, minute operations routine.

This "toe-to-toe" competition with diseases and disorders is even more remarkable when seen in a historical continuum. An astonishing amount of progress has been made in a very short time. Just two hundred years ago, the existence of germs as a cause of some diseases was unknown. In fact, it was less than 150 years ago that a British surgeon named Joseph Lister had difficulty persuading his fellow doctors that washing their hands before delivering a baby might increase the chances of a healthy delivery (especially if they had just attended to a diseased patient)!

Each book in Lucent's Diseases and Disorders series explores a disease or disorder and the knowledge that has been accumulated (or discarded) by doctors through the years. Each book also examines the tools used for pinpointing a diagnosis, as well as the various means that are used to treat or cure a disease. Finally, new ideas are presented—techniques or medicines that may be on the horizon.

Frustration and disappointment are still part of medicine, for not every disease or condition can be cured or prevented. But the limitations of knowledge are being pushed outward constantly; the "most difficult puzzles ever devised" are finding challengers every day.

A Common Illness

A GROUP OF STRANGERS with diverse backgrounds may not have much in common. But there is one thing that they all share. At some point in each of these individuals' lives, each has been or will be a victim of food poisoning. In fact, experts at the Centers for Disease Control estimate that each day two hundred thousand Americans come down with food poisoning. That translates to approximately one-quarter of all Americans annually. Most cases are mild and are commonly dismissed as a stomachache, which passes in a day. But sometimes when people eat food that contains harmful germs, the illness that follows can be very serious.

That is what happened to Laura, who at the time of her illness was an eighteen-year-old college freshman. She explains:

> My symptoms began with vomiting and diarrhea. Within two days, I could not tolerate water and the only thing coming out of my body was blood. A seven week hospitalization followed, during which I endured most medical treatments you could name and some you probably couldn't. . . . I spent Thanksgiving in intensive care with respiratory and kidney failure. As I lay comatose, on a respirator . . . my parents contemplated where I would be buried. That was not something we discussed when I left for college.[1]

Any Food Can Cause Problems

Fortunately, Laura survived her bout with food poisoning. And, although most of the 76 million reported food poisoning cases in the United States each year do not lead to hospitalization, about 325,000 cases do. Of these, the Centers for Disease Control estimate 2 to 3 percent cause long-term disability, with about 5,000 cases ending in death. Michael, the father of a two-year-old food poisoning victim explains: "I don't care how long I live, I will never believe my son died from eating a cheeseburger."[2]

It is not only burgers that can cause food poisoning. Almost every food can harbor food poisoning germs. Food poisoning cases have been linked to ice cream, rice, chicken, salad, melon, cereal, potatoes, soup, milk, juice, water, oysters, fish, sprouts, cheese, spices, chocolate, and eggs, to name just a few of the offenders.

It does not matter where a person eats, either. People have contracted food poisoning from food eaten at home, in restaurants, in school cafeterias, on picnics, at banquets, and even on luxury cruise ships.

Most victims of food poisoning suffer stomach discomfort like this teenage girl. Some victims, however, suffer severe symptoms that require medical attention.

The Cost

In addition to the potential cost of human lives, the financial cost of such a common disease is also high. According to the Economic Research Service of the U.S. Department of Agriculture (USDA) in 2003, food poisoning cases caused by the five most common foodborne germs cost approximately $6.9 billion. This includes medical costs, productivity losses due to missed workdays, and premature death. It does not include costs associated with other diseases that often arise as a complication of food poisoning. When these costs are factored in for just one type of foodborne bacteria, *Campylobacter jejuni*, the additional cost is estimated to be anywhere from $1.3 billion to $6 billion. Nor do these costs take into account the cost to food producers and processors when tainted food is recalled. For example, in 2002 more than 50 million pounds of beef were recalled at a retail cost of about three dollars per pound.

Lack of Knowledge

What makes matters worse, even though most food poisoning cases are preventable, many Americans do not possess enough knowledge about food safety to prevent them. The Food and Drug Administration's Center for Food Safety and Applied Nutrition compiled data from national surveys of American consumers and their knowledge of food safety issues. Findings of a 1995 survey, for example, revealed that one-third of 1,620 randomly selected individuals prepared food without taking precautions necessary to prevent food poisoning. Neglecting such precautions indicates a lack of knowledge of what these precautions are. Other surveys yielded similar results. The researchers concluded, "We find consumers have broad, moderate food safety concerns, [and] a wide but spotty understanding of foodborne illness prevention and consequences."[3]

Becoming Informed

Experts say that the consequences of food poisoning can be lessened. Most food poisoning cases are caused by mishaps along the food supply chain. These occur on the farm, in slaughterhouses, when food is packaged or distributed, as well as when

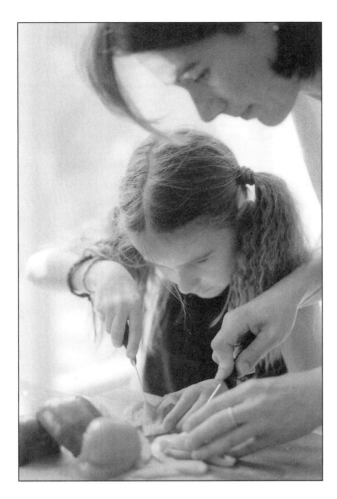

Applying simple food safety practices such as cutting vegetables on a clean surface with a clean knife can help prevent food poisoning.

food is stored or cooked. By learning about the infectious agents that cause food poisoning and how they spread, and by learning and following simple food safety and sanitary practices, individuals along every step of the food supply chain can take an active role in reducing the possibility of food becoming contaminated.

Indeed, when it comes to food poisoning the more knowledge an individual has, the less likely he or she will get sick. As food poisoning expert Nicols Fox explains, "Eating can—and certainly should—still be a pleasure. But information is power . . . armed with the facts individuals can apply what they know . . . to keep themselves and their families as safe as possible."[4]

Chapter 1

What Is Food Poisoning?

FOOD POISONING IS the term used to describe infections that occur when foods contaminated with disease-causing microorganisms known as pathogens are eaten. If food is not cooked thoroughly or handled properly, these pathogens infect people's digestive systems, causing an illness that is usually mild and short-term but at times can be life threatening.

Microorganisms, Helpful and Harmful

All microorganisms, including those that cause food poisoning, are creatures that are so small that they can be seen only through a microscope. Although invisible to the naked eye, they are found everywhere—in soil, water, and inside both animals' and humans' bodies. Some microorganisms are needed by the body to help it function properly. In fact, four hundred different types of bacteria live in a person's stomach and intestines where they, along with powerful acids, salts, and enzymes, break down food used to nourish the body.

Microorganisms that cause food poisoning are not in this group. These pathogens include bacteria, viruses, parasites, and mold. Like helpful bacteria, these harmful pathogens also live in the digestive tract of animals. In some cases the infected animals become sick, but often they do not. A person who consumes infected meat derived from these animals may become ill.

Pathogens can also pass through an animal's digestive tract and be shed in the animal's feces, which then contaminate any food the feces come in contact with. For example, when animals are slaughtered their intestines often burst. This allows microscopic bits of feces from the animal's large intestine to contaminate the rest of its body, which is then butchered for human consumption.

Pathogens in animal feces that are used as fertilizer can infect the soil as well as fruits and vegetables grown in that soil. Moreover, if contaminated feces pollute freshwater or salt water, the creatures that live in the water also become infected and so too do the individuals who eat them. Humans also can transmit pathogens through their feces. This may occur when fecal matter mixes with the water supply due to poor sewage, or when food handlers do not wash their hands after using the toilet.

Mold, on the other hand, forms when tiny spores that are found in and carried by air, water, and insects come in contact with moist food. Mold develops from these spores. As the mold grows, it spreads; becomes visible, and produces chemicals that make the infected food rot and cause food poisoning when eaten.

Microorganisms, like these paramecia magnified many times, exist everywhere. Although some microorganisms are beneficial to humans, many are harmful.

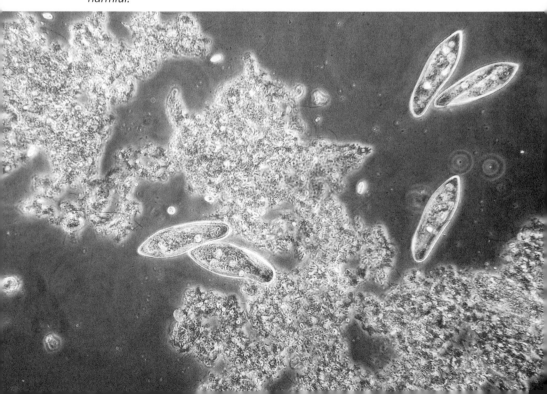

The Body Reacts

No matter the source, when a person eats contaminated food, digestive acids, enzymes, salts, and helpful bacteria go to work breaking down the infected food. Many pathogens do not survive this assault, but some do. Those that do take up residence in the victim's stomach and intestines multiply and produce toxins that make that person sick.

The toxins must be eliminated from the body before an infected person can get well. Therefore, the immune system sends white blood cells and powerful chemicals to the stomach and intestines to attack the infecting pathogens. This causes inflammation, which results in abdominal pain. At the same time, the brain signals nerves in the stomach to start the vomiting reflex. This causes nausea, which generally but not always leads to vomiting, a process in which digested and partially digested foods mixed with digestive fluids are expelled through the mouth.

In a further effort to eliminate the toxins, the brain directs the large intestine to secrete excess fluids. These are needed to break down the

A farmer spreads cow manure on his fields as fertilizer. Manure often contaminates the soil with harmful bacteria.

The Digestive System

The digestive tract is essentially a long pipe that goes from the mouth to the rectum. It allows food to pass through the body, be broken down into valuable nutrients, and for waste to be eliminated. The job of the digestive system is to turn food into nutrients that the body can use to feed itself. At the same time, chemicals in the digestive system work to destroy harmful microorganisms that can cause food poisoning.

Digestion begins in the mouth, where food is chewed up and mixes with saliva. Saliva contains antibodies and chemicals, called enzymes, which destroy germs. Once the food is swallowed, contracting muscles push the food down through the esophagus to the stomach. This process is called peristalsis.

Acids in the stomach break down the food and kill pathogens. The semidigested food then passes into the small intestine where enzymes complete the digestion process. Then the nutrients are absorbed into the bloodstream where they are carried to every cell in the body.

Waste products pass into the large intestine, or colon. Here water and electrolytes, which are a mixture of sodium and potassium, are removed, and the food becomes solid waste. This is excreted as feces from the body through the rectum.

infected food and toxins so they can be excreted from the body as feces. Excess fluids make the feces of a person with food poisoning extremely watery, which characterizes diarrhea. This process continually repeats itself until the body is rid of the infecting pathogens. Bill, a food poisoning victim explains: "I got diarrhea. And the diarrhea lasted for days and days—about a week in all."[5]

Complicating matters, some pathogens not only infect a person's digestive tract but pass into the victim's bloodstream where they are transported to other parts of the body. Food poisoning pathogens can infect an individual's liver, kidneys, lungs, heart, nerves, muscles, and bones. When this happens, food poisoning can be deadly.

Dangerous Bacteria

The most common food poisoning pathogens are bacteria. There are more than a dozen different species of bacteria that cause food poisoning and dozens of different strains of each kind of bacterium. Of these, *Campylobacter jejuni* is the most prevalent. It causes an estimated 4 million food poisoning cases and from two hundred to seven hundred deaths in the United States annually.

C. jejuni is found in the digestive tracts of cattle, pigs, sheep, goats, deer, wild birds, and poultry. Animals infected with the bacteria show no signs of illness, yet ongoing tests sponsored by the U.S. Department of Agriculture (USDA) show that 60 to 80 percent of all cattle and pigs harbor the pathogen, as do 90 percent of all poultry.

Dairy cows shed the bacteria in their milk. Although pasteurization destroys the bacteria, it is often found in unpasteurized or raw milk. In fact, in 1982 nineteen college students in Oregon contracted *Campylobacter* food poisoning from drinking unpasteurized milk. A similar outbreak occurred in 1985 in California when schoolchildren on a field trip to a dairy farm sampled raw milk. As a result, the Food and Drug Administration issued a warning advising school officials to prohibit students from sampling raw milk. John Sheehan, the director of the Food and Drug Administration's dairy and egg safety division, explains: "We continue to see outbreaks of food-borne illnesses associated with the consumption of raw milk every year. . . . It's pretty much the FDA's position that the health risks far outweigh the benefits [of drinking unpasteurized milk]."[6]

Unpasteurized milk can contain Campylobacter jejuni, *a bacterium shed by dairy cows that causes over 4 million food poisoning cases each year.*

Salmonella

Like *Campylobacter*, *Salmonella* is a very common pathogen. It causes an estimated 3 million cases of food poisoning a year. Since there are over two thousand different strains of *Salmonella*, this number is not surprising. Most commonly found in poultry and eggs, *Salmonella* infects the ovaries of seemingly healthy hens. There it is transmitted to eggs before the shell is even formed. In fact, according to the Centers for Disease Control, one out of every fifty Americans is exposed to a contaminated egg each year. Moreover, when tainted raw eggs are used as ingredients in other foods such as homemade ice cream, eggnog, powdered milk, cookie dough, and salad dressing, these foods also become contaminated. That is not all: Salmonellosis (the name of the disease caused by *Salmonella* bacteria) outbreaks have been linked to a wide variety of other foods including beef, cantaloupe, chocolate, cocoa, lamb, cheese, and yeast. Food experts say that these foods become contaminated after contact with infected feces.

David was among one hundred people who contracted salmonellosis after eating at a New York country club in June 2002. He describes his experience: "It was the best meal I've had . . . in a long time." However, two days later the vomiting and diarrhea began. David recalls: "I never had anything like this before. It was the worst feeling. I felt like I was totally lifeless. I couldn't move. I couldn't function. I couldn't even think straight."[7]

Pasteurization

Before 1860 the concept that heat destroyed pathogens that cause disease was unknown. The work of French scientist Louis Pasteur changed that. In Food Alert! *Morton Satin describes Pasteur's work:*

"He began to develop a strong sense that an intimate link existed between disease and the fermentation that accompanied the spoilage of food. In his drive to discover the causes of contagious diseases conclusively, Pasteur carried out in-depth research on the various causes of spoilage in wine, beer and vinegar. These studies eventually led to the investigation of disease in silkworms, and ultimately, to his probing analysis of human diseases. Pasteur's untiring efforts eventually revolutionized the medical world and are undeniably among the most important scientific works to benefit mankind. For the first time, a sound theoretical basis for controlling microorganisms and their effects had been established.

During 1860–1864, Pasteur showed that wine spoilage resulted from simple microbial metabolisms. To control the

E. coli

Escherichia coli, or *E. coli*, is another leading cause of food poisoning. According to the Centers for Disease Control, just one strain of this bacteria, *E. coli* O157:H7, is estimated to cause twenty thousand cases of food poisoning in the United States each year. Because it often spreads to a victim's kidneys, *E. coli* O157:H7 kills about five hundred people annually.

problem, he suggested a low level of heat treatment, which was enough to deactivate the spoilage microorganisms (122–140 degrees F or 50–60 degrees C) but not enough to damage the quality or character of the finished wine. This was, and still is, the key to the pasteurization process. While he could easily have boiled the wine vigorously to kill off all the microorganisms, that would have affected the wine's taste as well. . . . He therefore set about to determine the absolute minimum temperatures required to accomplish the job without wrecking the product's traditional character. The final pasteurization technique was so effective, it was quickly applied to beer and vinegar products as well. . . .

For the first time in history, a simple method was available to prevent the sort of spoilage that had always been considered a sad, but natural, fact of life. . . . Wine and beer may not be absolutely essential for life but, as far as children are concerned, milk is what is important. Thus, in the field of public health, the benefits of pasteurization were greatest. Even though Pasteur himself did not apply his technique to milk, this new method achieved its greatest success in the dairy industry. When the process was eventually applied to milk [in 1880], it was christened pasteurization in due recognition of Pasteur's unequaled contribution to science, health and humanity."

Found in tainted ground beef such as hamburger, the E. coli *bacterium is a leading cause of food poisoning in the United States.*

Found in most animals' digestive tracts, *E. coli* has been implicated in the contamination of fruits and vegetables fertilized with infected manure, but it is most frequently transmitted in ground beef. This is because when meat is ground, the grinding process spreads bacteria. According to the U.S. Department of Agriculture, 89 percent of ground beef used in hamburgers contains some *E. coli* O157:H7. USDA epidemiologist Mark Powell explains: "The bottom line is that *E. coli* O157:H7 is pretty ubiquitous in ground beef."[8]

Therefore, it is not surprising that hamburgers are often suspected in *E. coli* cases. A mother recalls her doctor's reaction when her son, Damion, was infected with *E.coli*: "Dr. Kelton's first question, when he heard of Damion's illness was, So when did he eat the hamburger?"[9]

Outbreaks of illness caused by *E. coli* and traced to tainted hamburgers have been reported in the United States since the 1980s. One of the biggest outbreaks occurred in 1993, when 795 people in five states got sick and four children died after eating contaminated burgers purchased at Jack in the Box restaurants.

Parasites and Mold

Parasites and mold also cause problems. Mold can produce a toxin called mycotoxin, which when consumed causes food poisoning. Mold can live on animal and plant products. It is most commonly found on fruit, grains, or nuts, as well as on foods that have passed their prime. Moisture of any kind can cause mold to form. In fact, a 1992 food poisoning epidemic in China occurred after one hundred people ate rice that had become moldy because of continuous rainfall during the rice harvest.

Parasites also cause food poisoning. The most common parasites are protozoa, one-celled animals that reside in water contaminated with fecal matter. When fruits and vegetables are irrigated with this water, they become contaminated. Other parasites linked to food poisoning include *Trichinella spiralis*, a microscopic worm that lives in the intestines of pigs, horses, and wild animals. It is transmitted to humans when they eat infected meat. Food expert Morton Satin describes what happened to a group of people who ate sausages infected with *T. spiralis*: "Within a short period, members of three related families came down with trichinellosis. All had diarrhea as well as severe muscular and abdominal pains. The most severe case, a 55 year old woman, became feverish and had to be hospitalized. After almost three weeks in the hospital she developed bronchopneumonia and died. An autopsy revealed several muscle samples containing *Trichinella*.[10]

Viruses

Viruses can also be transmitted in food. Two of the most common foodborne viruses are hepatitis A and the Norwalk virus. In fact, the Norwalk virus is responsible for an estimated 181,000 cases of food poisoning each year. Both the Norwalk and hepatitis A viruses are spread through fecal matter. These viruses frequently infect produce irrigated with tainted water. A 2003 hepatitis A outbreak in Pennsylvania in which green onions sickened five hundred people is linked to this practice. So too is a 1997 hepatitis A outbreak in Michigan, which sickened hundreds of children who ate strawberries as part of a school lunch program. Sue, whose daughter Lindsay was among the victims, recalls: "Lindsay was hospitalized after she spent three days with severe abdominal cramps, vomiting, fever, and a splitting headache. She refused to eat or drink. She didn't want to go to the hospital because it hurt to move. I have never seen a child so sick."[11]

Even more frequently, these viruses infect shellfish such as oysters, mussels, clams, crabs, and lobsters. The virus gains entrance through openings in the creatures' shells. Infected shellfish caused a 1988 hepatitis A epidemic in China that affected sixteen thousand people.

Another outbreak occurred in 2002, when almost one-third of the 550 Academy of Motion Picture Arts and Sciences' Scientific and Technical Award nominees came down with food poisoning. The culprit was lobster that carried the Norwalk virus. This outbreak, as well as a 1993 outbreak that sickened 127 Americans who ate raw oysters infected with the Norwalk virus, was traced to the practice of flushing waste from toilets on fishing boats directly into the sea.

Outbreaks of viral diseases are often widespread because infected people can infect others through person-to-person contact or through things they have touched. Therefore, such outbreaks frequently occur in places where many people are in close contact, such as on cruise ships. In 2002 alone more than nine hundred cruise ship passengers fell ill from the Norwalk virus. And in 2003 a cruise ship headed for Europe was forced to cut short the voyage and return to New York in order to allow three hundred ill passengers to disembark.

Conditions That Lead to Food Poisoning

No matter what pathogen infects food or in what circumstances a person contracts food poisoning, cases of food poisoning have been on the increase since the 1980s. Experts theorize that there is a connection between this increase and changes in the food industry. These include the global distribution of food, factory farming, and inappropriate food handling.

In the past most available food—fruits and vegetables in particular—were locally grown. In the 1950s, for example, American supermarkets offered about three hundred food items for sale. Fruits and vegetables were sold only during the season in which they were harvested. Today large supermarkets offer as many as fifty thousand food products, many of which are imported. For example, out-of-season fruits imported from Latin America are commonly sold year-round in American supermarkets. Indeed, a typical supermarket sells produce from twenty-six different countries.

Traps like these are used to catch lobsters. Lobsters and other shellfish are often infected with viruses that cause food poisoning.

Although having a wide variety of food choices has its benefits, there are also drawbacks. Food is only as safe as the environment it comes from. Nicols Fox explains: "When we consume this produce we forget that we are, in essence, consuming the soil and water in which they were grown and even the working, living, and sanitation conditions of those who picked and packed the products. Whether those harvesters have access to bathroom and hand-washing facilities can suddenly become very important when we eat the produce."[12]

An American who lived in Colombia explains:

> I love my fruit. But when I went to the grocery store in Colombia, the local people told me that I shouldn't touch the fruit and vegetables because they still had mud and fertilizer on them that would make me sick. When I got the fruit home, I had to scrub everything real well. They said to use bleach because of all the stuff on the fruits and because the tap water was dirty.

Modern supermarkets carry food items from around the world that can carry a wide variety of pathogens.

Now when I see imported fruit in the U.S., I figure that the local stores clean it because the local stores don't want people getting sick. Plus, Americans won't buy food that looks dirty. Americans want food that looks clean and attractive. But even so, I remember the grocery stores in Colombia, and when I buy imported fruit I scrub it extra well when I get it home.[13]

Many Americans do not scrub imported fruits. They assume that American supermarkets thoroughly clean these items before displaying them. But this assumption is incorrect. Supermarkets routinely spray all produce with water. However, microscopic contaminents cannot always be removed in this manner and may still cling to the products' skin. Consequently, it is not unexpected that a number of recent food poisoning cases, including the 2003 and 1997 hepatitis A outbreaks mentioned earlier, have been linked to imported berries, onions, melons, tomatoes, and sprouts.

Factory Farming and Processing

Modern factory farming methods are also linked to food poisoning. Unlike small family-run farms of the past, modern farms are big businesses where large numbers of animals are crowded into small areas. For instance, a modern chicken farm has anywhere from thirty thousand to one hundred thousand chickens housed in close quarters. With so many animals it is almost inevitable that infected feces will get mixed in with animal feed and water. This causes whole flocks to rapidly become infected. Some experts say that this is one reason so many chickens are infected with *Campylobacter* and *Salmonella* bacteria.

Moreover, once chickens are slaughtered their feathers are removed mechanically. The machine that does this resembles a set of fast-moving rubber fingers. Unfortunately, this machine can spread pathogens. With repeated use, the rubber fingers tend to crack. Pathogens get in the cracks and are transmitted from bird to bird. This is an especial problem because *Campylobacter* bacteria thrive in empty feather follicles.

Bacteria are also transmitted when machines gut the chickens, causing the intestines to rupture. Finally, in order to add water weight to the chickens so they can be sold for a higher price, chicken carcasses are placed in large vats of cold water for an hour. Cold water does not destroy bacteria. Instead, bacteria spread rapidly from carcass to carcass in this chill bath. Indeed, former USDA microbiologist Gerald Kuester describes the results of this process: "The final product is no different than if you stuck it [the chicken] in the toilet and ate it."[14]

Beef and pig farms are also raising more animals in less space, which allows infection to spread easily from animal to animal. As with chickens, the processing of these animals has changed. It is common for cattle to be packed together and left to fast for a day before they are slaughtered. This is done so the animals can empty their intestines. However, this procedure stresses the cattle, which makes them shed more bacteria than usual in their feces. Because of the small quarters the animals are kept in, they often wind up standing in each other's feces. It is not uncommon for microscopic bits of feces to stick to their skin and for pathogens to enter their bodies through their pores. Also, faster slaughtering methods, which allow as many as three hundred cows to be slaughtered within an hour, increase the possibility of fecal matter getting on the slaughtering tools and being transferred from cow to cow. Mark, a biologist, explains: "It's the machines. They operate at such a speed that it is almost impossible to avoid infection. The bacteria are on the animals' skins. Then the bacteria get on the machines and are processed into the animals. People don't know it, they eat the meat and they get a stomachache."[15]

Complicating matters, ground beef is not made from one particular cow. It is not unusual for meat from one hundred cows to be found in one hamburger. Pathogens from one contaminated cow can infect the meat from uninfected cows when the meat is mixed together and ground. In fact, according to the USDA, one infected cow can contaminate sixteen tons of ground beef. Centers for Disease Control microbiologist Gregory Armstrong explains: "Increased use of large production lots for products such as hamburger may . . . provide a setting in which . . . pathogens can rapidly move into human populations."[16]

Chicken farms often raise the birds in tightly packed pens like these. Such conditions allow infections to spread easily among the chickens.

Unsafe Food Handling

The way food is handled can also lead to infection. It is true that unsafe food handling has always caused food poisoning, but this used to occur mainly in the home and affected the people who lived there. Today, however, with more people eating in restaurants as well as purchasing prepared take-out foods, unsafe food handling practices are affecting larger groups of people rather than just individual families.

One problem is that food handlers in most restaurants receive limited training that does not always provide them with the knowledge they need to protect the public. As a result, food handlers are often more careless than they might otherwise be if they were more aware of the problems their behavior can cause. Indeed, a November 2003 hidden camera investigation by *Dateline NBC* of one thousand fast-food restaurants in thirty-eight states found food handlers committing a multitude of unsafe food handling practices. These included employees using dirty food preparation counters, cooking foods at temperatures too low to destroy bacteria, leaving cooked food out in the open for extended periods of time, and combining raw meat with cooked

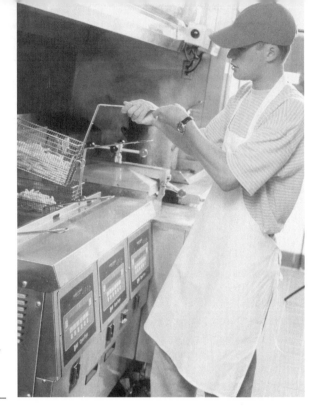

Fast-food workers sometimes handle food without regard to public health. The fast-food industry has been blamed for a number of food poisoning cases.

meat, all of which can cause food poisoning. In addition, the investigation found that it was quite common for food handlers to touch ready-to-eat food with their bare, unwashed hands. In fact, the cameras found one food handler scooping ice into a drink cup with his hands.

Such practices are not limited to fast-food restaurants. A New Yorker describes her experience at a take-out store:

> I stopped in a take-out store for a container of chicken noodle soup to take out for lunch. The man behind the counter used a ladle to dish out the soup. When I asked for more noodles, he put his hand into the soup pot and grabbed a handful of noodles. I left the soup on the counter. It was a good thing I was watching, or I'd have bought the soup, eaten it, and probably got sick.[17]

It is apparent that food becomes contaminated when it is infected with one of a number of different pathogens. Conditions like unsafe food handling, factory farming, and the global distribution of food contribute to this process. But no matter which pathogen causes or what conditions contribute to food contamination, when people eat tainted food, the result is usually food poisoning.

Chapter 2

Diagnosis and Treatment

WHEN OTHERWISE HEALTHY people complain of abdominal pain and/or nausea, vomiting, or diarrhea, the cause of these symptoms is usually food poisoning. In many cases individuals can be treated without medication and their symptoms will resolve on their own. However, if food poisoning symptoms persist for more than three days, if they worsen, or if new symptoms such as bloody diarrhea and fever occur, medication may be needed. Moreover, when food poisoning pathogens damage other parts of the body, causing complications, urgent lifesaving treatment is called for. No matter what form of treatment is administered, the goal is to eliminate the infecting pathogens and toxins from the body. How this goal is met depends on the particular pathogen and the severity of the problem.

A Diagnosis Based on the Symptoms

Making a general diagnosis of food poisoning is not difficult. Although individuals suffering from indigestion or an upset stomach may complain of nausea, vomiting, abdominal pain, and diarrhea, in food poisoning the symptoms are more pronounced. For instance, in food poisoning forceful waves of stomach pain followed by vomiting and/or diarrhea usually occur every fifteen minutes to an hour with the consistency of the diarrhea becoming progressively looser and more watery as time goes on. The stomach pain of indigestion or an upset stomach, on the other hand, is less intense and is generally followed by only one or two episodes of vomiting or diarrhea. Bonnie, a health care professional explains: "Food poisoning makes you so sick that it's easy to tell the difference between it and a bad stomach. With food poisoning, stomach cramps can have you doubled over with pain. You are repeatedly retching and emptying your bowels. That doesn't happen with an upset stomach."[18] Moreover, in food poisoning it is not uncommon for large groups of people who have all eaten infected food to become ill. This does not occur in cases of indigestion or upset stomachs.

Depending on the pathogen, food poisoning symptoms can develop anywhere from two hours to seven weeks after a person eats infected food. For example, symptoms of salmonellosis generally appear between twelve and seventy-two hours after an individual has eaten contaminated food, but symptoms of hepatitis A

A doctor examines a patient complaining of abdominal pains. Because her symptoms appear mild, the doctor will probably rule out food poisoning.

do not appear for about a month. Even though each pathogen has its own time frame, most food poisoning symptoms develop in one to three days after a person has eaten contaminated food. Those symptoms usually disappear when infecting pathogens have been eliminated from the body. This generally takes no more than three days.

Sometimes, however, symptoms can persist for weeks. When this occurs, due to repeated vomiting and diarrhea, patients can lose too many fluids, salts, and chemicals known as electrolytes from their bodies. This leads to dehydration, which is characterized by dry and cracked skin and lips, excessive thirst, inability to urinate, lethargy, confusion, irrational behavior, and hallucinations. Nicols Fox describes how dehydration affected a food poisoning victim: "After prolonged, persistent diarrhea, . . . she knew she was acting strangely and knew she needed fluids, but she simply no longer cared. When she was taken to the hospital she was found to be severely dehydrated."[19]

Fluids, salts, and electrolytes that have been lost as a result of dehydration must be replaced. Otherwise insufficient water in an individual's blood can lead to shock and death. Therefore, food poisoning victims who are suffering from dehydration need medical attention. Severely dehydrated patients are hospitalized and administered fluid intravenously until they are rehydrated.

In addition to dehydration, other symptoms also indicate that medical treatment is needed. These include blood-laced diarrhea, muscle pain, fever, chills, and headaches. Blood-laced diarrhea, in particular, is associated with *Campylobacter*, *Salmonella*, *E. coli*, and *Staphylococcus* bacteria; the hepatitis A virus; and anisakid parasites. It is an indication that food poisoning pathogens are destroying cells in the digestive tract. When this occurs it is not uncommon for the pathogens to spread into the victim's bloodstream, where they can cause problems throughout the body. Blood-laced diarrhea also points to the possibility of rips in the patient's colon caused by frequent diarrhea.

Complicating matters, the symptoms of infection with some rare pathogens are atypical. Foodborne botulism, caused by *Clostridium botulinum*, a lethal bacteria that develops in improperly canned foods, does not cause nausea, vomiting, or diarrhea. Instead it paralyzes muscles and nerves. If it is not treated, it can result in death. Since different pathogens require different treatments, tests may be administered to identify the infecting pathogen. Taking a stool culture is the most common way to do this.

Testing

Taking a stool culture involves patients providing a sample of their feces for analysis. This entails patients moving their bowels into a specimen cup. Darrylyn, who was hospitalized due to a severe case of hemorrhagic colitis caused by *E. coli* poisoning, recalls: "I had the urge to go to the bathroom. . . . They put a plastic cup in the toilet to catch everything. . . . I gave the hospital the specimen it needed."[20]

Once the specimen is taken, it is sent to a laboratory where it is examined under a microscope. Worms and other parasites can easily be identified in this manner. Different species of bacteria can also be distinguished by their size, shape, and by the way they move. However, different strains of each bacteria are more difficult to identify.

Viruses are more difficult to identify because they are extremely small. In order to be identified, viruses must be viewed under a high-powered electron microscope, which is not commonly found in local medical laboratories. Therefore, viral pathogens in stool cultures frequently go undetected.

Despite these drawbacks, a stool culture is important. Identifying some pathogens, such as *Clostridium botulinum*, can save a patient's life. Once *C. botulinum* is identified, a lifesaving antitoxin vaccine that counteracts the effect of the pathogen is quickly administered.

Results of a stool culture also help doctors determine whether or not antibiotics should be administered. This is because antibiotics are effective in destroying some bacteria and parasites, but have no effect on viruses.

Besides a stool culture, the doctor may request a sample of the suspected food. If it is available, it too is sent to a laboratory for analysis. Besides helping to identify the offending pathogen, once it is determined that a food item is indeed infected, public health agencies can begin tracking down where the food came from and where it was distributed. Once this is determined, businesses where the food is sold are notified and the infected food is removed from the food supply. This process helps prevent a food poisoning epidemic.

Intravenous fluids are often administered to victims of food poisoning to counter severe dehydration from diarrhea and vomiting.

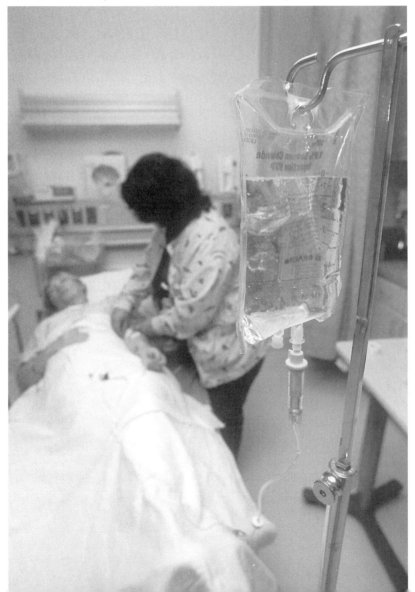

Botulism

Botulism is one of the most dangerous forms of food poisoning. In Spoiled: Why Our Food Is Making Us Sick and What We Can Do About It, *Nicols Fox discusses this disease.*

"Botulism is an extremely serious disease. It begins with difficulty swallowing and double vision that may or may not be accompanied by vomiting and muscle weakness; it then develops into a descending paralysis. The fatality rate is 7.5 to 10 percent. Often misdiagnosed, botulism is treated with an antitoxin that can be obtained only from the CDC [Centers for Disease Control]. Since that agency carefully tracks those requests, it is one disease for which there are pretty good numbers—except for those cases that are never diagnosed.

When home canning was more widely practiced, botulism was a real danger. The spores of *Clostridium botulinium* are found in the ground, and since plants are grown in soil, the spores are frequently found on vegetables. In the

Home Treatment

Even when patients seek medical treatment and the infecting pathogen has been identified, if the patient's symptoms are not prolonged or severe or if the infecting pathogen is a virus, medication may not be called for. In mild cases of food poisoning, while the digestive system is eliminating the infecting pathogen from the body via diarrhea and vomiting, the goal of treatment is to avoid dehydration. This involves replacing lost fluids, salts, and electrolytes. Drinking any noncaffeinated liquid is helpful. Caffeinated beverages are avoided because they can irritate the digestive tract and increase abdominal cramps and contractions.

normal course of food preparation, vegetables are eaten before the spores develop and produce toxin. Unfortunately, the conditions preferred by *C. botulinum*, low oxygen and low acid are perfectly met in home-canned low-acid foods that may not have been processed long enough at high enough temperatures to destroy the spores. . . .

Ironically, it is quite often consumer demand that sets the stage for foodborne illness. People like sweet foods, and growers have obliged by selectively breeding for sweeter and lower-acid tomatoes. Tomatoes used to be a staple for home canners precisely because they were acidic enough to resist the growth of *C. botulinum*. While it might have been dicey canning beans, a non-acid food, one could be certain that the acidity in tomatoes would prevent the unseen, odorless toxin production of *C. botulinum*. . . . That guarantee for home canners has now disappeared. Several outbreaks of botulism have been caused by salsa made with the new varieties of tomatoes that are less acidic and therefore less able to retard the growth of the pathogen."

The Gatorade type of sports drink, which contains electrolytes and sodium, is especially effective.

Patients are directed to drink one cup of fluid per hour throughout the first day of illness. Since it is often difficult for an individual with food poisoning to keep even a cup of liquid down, patients are advised to take small sips, which are more likely to stay down than large gulps. If this does not work, patients often suck on ice chips until they are able to successfully keep down fluids. In addition, solid food is avoided on the first day. Eating solid food taxes the patient's already overworked digestive system.

On the second day patients are generally allowed to eat solid food. Foods like crackers, dry toast, clear soup, and flavored gelatin are the first to be introduced since they are easy to digest. They are often followed by other easily digestible foods such as baked potatoes, bananas, steamed fish, skinless chicken, and cooked vegetables. Spicy or fatty foods and dairy products are avoided because they are difficult to digest. At the same time, patients continue drinking at least one cup of noncaffeinated liquid every hour.

Of course, while people are suffering from food poisoning they are generally too weak to go to work or school. They need to get plenty of rest in order to strengthen their bodies. John, a food poisoning victim, recalls: "I felt crummy. My stomach felt sour. I had

Even mild cases of food poisoning can make the victim weak and uncomfortable. Bed rest may be needed to help regain strength.

diarrhea repeatedly. I felt real bad, kind of achy all over. I didn't go to work. I couldn't, even if I'd wanted to. I stayed close to the toilet, rested, and drank gallons of Seven-Up."[21]

Antacids and Antidiarrheal Medicines

In addition to drinking plenty of fluids, modifying their diets, and resting, some people with food poisoning turn to over-the-counter medications in hopes of lessening their symptoms. These medications include antidiarrheal drugs and antacids.

Antidiarrheal medicines contain absorbents that soak up liquids in the digestive tract. This thickens and hardens the consistency of the feces, slowing down their movement through the large intestine and colon and thus lessening diarrhea episodes. However, as unpleasant as diarrhea is, it is the body's way to rid itself of infecting pathogens. Therefore, most experts do not recommend that people with food poisoning take antidiarrheal medicine.

Antacids are another popular over-the-counter medication. They reduce the production of stomach acids. This lessens feelings of indigestion and nausea. Despite these benefits, taking antacids can actually worsen a person's symptoms. Stomach acids are needed to break down infected food so that it can be eliminated from the body. Slowing down this process can prolong a bout of food poisoning. Furthermore, chemicals in stomach acids, kill many pathogens. By decreasing the production of stomach acids, pathogens that otherwise might have been destroyed are allowed to survive. This can turn a mild case of food poisoning into a severe case. Bill, who was hospitalized when his salmonellosis symptoms worsened explains:

> Before and during the early stages of this disease, I had been taking antacids. What I didn't know—what many millions of Americans still don't know—is that antacids weaken a person's ability to prevent food-borne illnesses. The acid in our stomachs helps kill microbes. Not always, not thoroughly, but stomach acid plays a major role in thwarting infection. A bright infectious disease specialist uncovered that risk factor for me.[22]

When Prescription Drugs Are Needed

When food poisoning symptoms do not resolve on their own, or when symptoms worsen, patients may need medication. Antibiotics are the most common drugs prescribed for food poisoning. They are used in treating illnesses caused by bacteria and some parasites but are ineffective against viruses and worms. Antibiotics include drugs such as penicillin and tetracycline. Chemicals in antibiotics attack and destroy bacteria and parasites. This includes both harmful and helpful bacteria. Since helpful bacteria take up space in the digestive tract, which keeps harmful bacteria from taking up residence, antibiotics are used only when dietary modification, fluid replacement, and rest prove to be ineffective. Complicating matters, not all bacteria respond to antibiotic treatment. Because of mutations in their makeup, some forms of bacteria, such as *E. coli* O157:H7, are resistant to antibiotics. The resistant pathogens are not affected when an antibiotic is administered. Instead, helpful bacteria are destroyed and the pathogens quickly take root in their place, causing the infection to worsen. This happened to Cynthia, who was infected with a resistant form of *Salmonella*. When she was administered an antibiotic,

> Her illness was first severe, then she got better, then much, much worse. In hindsight the antibiotic she was given was probably the reason. It didn't touch the resistant bacteria but wiped out all the competition that had been keeping it in some kind of check. The pain she remembers was unbelievable: "I can't begin to tell you how many times I was up during the night. I couldn't keep a thing down."[23]

Alternative Treatments

Because antibiotics can destroy helpful bacteria, some people turn to alternative treatments as a substitute for antibiotics or as a way to balance the ill effects that antibiotics can cause. Unlike traditional medicines, alternative treatments have not been widely studied and are not regulated by the U.S. government.

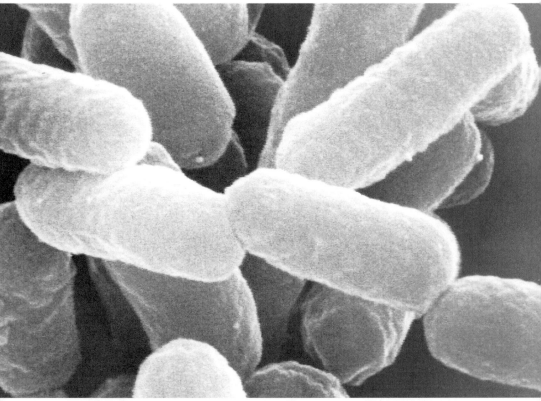

E. coli *O157:H7 bacteria, here magnified many times, are resistant to antibiotics. This means they can survive antibiotic treatment while beneficial bacteria are destroyed.*

Alternative treatments for food poisoning involve the use of natural substances that are believed to detoxify the body. These include charcoal tablets, garlic capsules, herbal teas, and yogurt.

Yogurt is often combined with antibiotics to treat food poisoning. It has been used as a digestive aid for many years in Europe. Yogurt contains helpful live *Lactobacillus* bacteria. When yogurt is taken with antibiotics, it is thought that *Lactobacillus* competes with and displaces harmful food poisoning bacteria in an infected person's digestive tract. However, because dairy products are often difficult to digest, some people take *Lactobacillus* in capsule form.

There are few studies to support the effectiveness of *Lacto-bacillus*, but many people find it beneficial and many experts agree. Nicols Fox explains: "Anecdotal reports, long experience in Europe, and common sense in understanding the theory of 'competitive exclusion,' whereby the gut is reinforced with 'good bacteria' would lead one to try this method."[24]

Garlic capsules are another alternative treatment. They are often used in place of antibiotics. Garlic has long been known to have antibacterial properties. Proponents of garlic treatment say that when it is taken for food poisoning, it detoxifies the digestive tract by destroying harmful bacteria. The herb goldenseal is also thought to be a natural antibiotic. It is usually taken in tea or in capsule form. However, problems can arise

Yogurt is a common source of beneficial bacteria that can help fight disease-causing microorganisms in the digestive tract.

because both garlic and goldenseal can be difficult to digest. Therefore, their use may create an additional burden on an already overworked digestive tract, causing stomach cramps and indigestion. John explains: "I took garlic capsules because they were supposed to kill bad bacteria. They made me nauseous, and gassy, and gave me really fragrant garlic burps. That didn't help my stomach."[25]

Charcoal tablets are another popular substitute for antibiotics. Charcoal tablets are made from activated charcoal, which is extremely absorbent. When a charcoal tablet enters a person's digestive tract it acts like a sponge. Although it is theorized that charcoal absorbs poisons in the digestive tract, thus ridding the body of harmful pathogens, it also absorbs digestive liquids, vital nutrients, and helpful bacteria. For this reason, although some people feel that charcoal tablets are beneficial, many health experts say that using charcoal tablets to relieve the symptoms of food poisoning is risky.

Treating Complications

When pathogens travel through a victim's bloodstream and damage other parts of his or her body, neither traditional nor alternative treatments can prevent the possibility of long-term damage or death occurring. In these cases patients must be hospitalized, and depending on the organs affected, other treatments are administered. The most common complication caused by severe food poisoning is hemolytic uremic syndrome, or HUS. HUS occurs when food poisoning pathogens and toxins get into a person's bloodstream where they shred white blood cells sent to attack them. The white blood cells are carried to the kidneys, through which fluid waste is ordinarily eliminated from the body as urine. However, the shredded cells clog the kidneys, and fluid waste cannot be released. The patient's body becomes swollen, and if the fluid is not eliminated, the patient can die. Serena, a HUS survivor recalls: "My body was grotesquely swollen from the fluids my kidneys could not excrete. I was so bloated that I couldn't even bend my fingers and it felt as if my skin might burst."[26]

As more and more white blood cells are destroyed, other organs such as the liver, lungs, and heart also become clogged. This prevents them from functioning effectively and can cause these organs to fail. When this occurs, death follows. Those who survive are often left with permanent kidney, lung, liver, and digestive tract damage.

There is no preferred treatment for people with HUS. As in all cases of food poisoning, in order for symptoms to cease the infection has to be eliminated from the victim's body. Therefore, if the infecting pathogen responds to an antibiotic, the medication is administered intravenously. But since most cases of HUS are caused by resistant *E. coli* O157:H7, antibiotics are not usually prescribed. Instead, treatment for HUS involves supporting the failing organs until the infection runs its course. Accordingly, to support failing kidneys, HUS patients are attached to a kidney dialysis machine that filters fluid out of the kidneys. They are given plasma and blood transfusions in order to replace shredded white blood cells. If the lungs are infected, patients are attached to a respirator to help them breathe more easily. Serena explains:

> I was in the hospital for almost three weeks. Most of that time, in excruciating pain. The tubes seemed to come out of everywhere. I spent hours at a time hooked up to a plasmapheresis [a plasma replacement machine] and dialysis machines, wondering if my life could ever be the same again. It was so hard to believe that my entire life had been turned upside down by a hamburger.[27]

HUS is not the only complication that severe food poisoning can cause. Although it is uncommon, food poisoning pathogens can infect a patient's joints, causing a form of arthritis known as reactive arthritis. In most cases the infecting pathogen is *Campylobacter jejuni*. Usually, treatment with antibiotics and anti-inflammatory drugs that reduce swelling in the joints cures reactive arthritis.

Similarly, if *C. jejuni* spreads to a person's nervous system it can cause Guillain-Barré syndrome, an illness that causes paralysis throughout the body. Although in most cases the paralysis eventually disappears, it can take months for this to happen, and some cases never heal. The likelihood that an individual infected with *C. jejuni* will develop Guillain-Barré syndrome is rare. The syndrome occurs in one out of every thousand cases of *C. jejuni* food poisoning.

People at Risk

Although complications can arise in any food poisoning case, they are more likely to occur in people who have weak immune systems and are, therefore, less able to fight off the effects of pathogens. These include children under age five, the elderly,

Kidney dialysis is often needed in cases of HUS to help overworked kidneys excrete fluids and toxins.

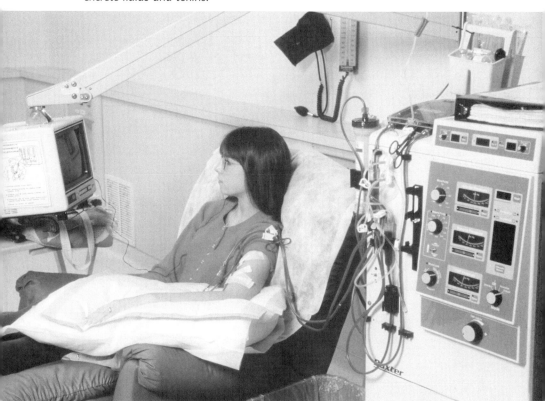

When *Listeria* Strikes

Julia Capriotti has cerebral palsy, which she contracted as a fetus when her pregnant mother ate contaminated food. A June 4, 2003, article by Aparna Surendran appearing in Penn State University's Centre Daily Times *describes what happened to Julia.*

"Julia, 5, who stands 3 feet tall and weighs 25 pounds, has cerebral palsy. She can't walk or stand on her own. She has difficulty using her right hand and needs speech, physical and occupational therapy.

Julia's problem began before she was born.

Her mother, Lynn Nowak, was 26½ weeks pregnant when she began experiencing flu-like symptoms on Sept. 2, 1997. She had body aches, chills, a 102 degree fever and a terrible headache. By midnight, she could no longer feel her baby move inside her.

The next day, an ultrasound revealed that the baby had a high heartbeat but was not moving. The doctor said the baby most likely had an infection, and they would have to deliver immediately.

Doctors took Julia by Caesarean section early the following morning. She weighed 2 pounds, 2 ounces. She hovered near death; a priest was called to give the baby last rites.

Julia survived, but her esophagus was torn; she had bleeding in her brain, which obstructed the flow of cerebrospinal fluid; and she had heart problems. All of this, the doctors said, was due to something the Capriotti family had never heard of—Listeria monocytogenes, a food-borne pathogen associated particularly with precooked meats. . . .

Julia came home for good on New Year's day 1998, but she could not sit up by herself. When she was about a year old, her neurologist said she had cerebral palsy.

'I was scared; I felt guilty' Nowak said. 'I was just glad to have this little girl, (but) I ate whatever caused this.'"

pregnant women, and people suffering from HIV, cancer, and other illnesses. Elton, a food poisoning victim, explains: "I was the only one in my family to get food poisoning although we all ate the same food. I bet it was because I had polio [a serious illness], and the rest of my family was stronger."[28]

Pregnant women, in particular, are especially vulnerable to the effects of food poisoning. A woman's immune system weakens during pregnancy in order to protect the fetus from being rejected as a foreign object that endangers the mother's body. Infection with *Listeria monocytogenes*, a food poisoning bacteria that causes an illness called listeriosis and is often found in lunch meats and soft cheese, is especially dangerous for pregnant women. Pregnant women are twenty times more likely to contract listeriosis than other adults. And, because whatever a pregnant woman eats or drinks is passed on to the fetus through the placenta, the fetus also becomes infected. This can cause a miscarriage or stillbirth. Listeriosis is such a threat to the welfare of unborn babies that in 1992 the Centers for Disease Control issued a warning advising pregnant women to avoid eating cold cuts. Laureen, who miscarried her baby due to listeriosis, explains: "On October 5th, 2000 I miscarried a perfectly healthy baby girl. I was thirteen weeks pregnant. At the hospital, the doctor told me they suspected listeria, a bacterial infection. Later that day, it was confirmed that that is what caused me to lose the baby. . . . Everyday I wonder what it is that I ate that killed our little girl."[29]

Babies that do survive *L. monocytogenes* infection are often born prematurely. Some have meningitis, an infection of the brain, which is caused when *Listeria* bacteria infect the baby's central nervous system. Prompt treatment with antibiotics can destroy these pathogens and save the baby's life.

Fortunately, not every case of food poisoning threatens the lives of babies or other victims. Whether or not medication is administered depends on the severity of the illness as well as the infecting pathogen. But no matter what treatment is prescribed, eliminating the pathogen from the patient's body provides the victim with relief.

Chapter 3

Avoiding Food Poisoning

IT IS NOT ALWAYS possible to avoid a case of food poisoning, but experts agree that people can lessen their chance of infection by taking precautionary steps. These include practicing safe food handling, preparation, and storage at home, as well as being aware of and avoiding unsafe food practices in stores and restaurants.

Shopping for Food

The first step consumers can take in protecting themselves from infection is deciding where to shop for food. It is important that stores are clean. According to David Nash of the American Food Safety Institute, "Overall sanitation is an indicator of how much they [the store's management and workforce] care, if they care about you as a customer and if they care about food safety, they will make a good attempt to keep the place clean."[30]

One sign that a store is clean is if it free of insects and rodents. Rodents can transmit viruses and bacteria in their feces, and insects can transmit parasites in their eggs. Insects often lay their eggs on overripe fruit. Once the fruit is eaten the eggs develop into larvae or tiny worms in the victim's intestines, causing food poisoning symptoms. Morton Satin describes one such case: "A Washington mother of a one-year-old girl frequently saw worms in her child's stool. . . . Probing into the child's dietary history showed that she had been fed over-ripe bananas that had been kept in a wire basket. . . . Flies were regularly swarming around the fruit basket."[31] In addition, insects transmit spores from which mold develops. This causes food to rot and spreads dangerous toxins.

Of course, store employees should also be clean. Experts recommend that food handlers wear a protective hat or hairnet to keep dry skin that sheds from the scalp and parasites that shelter in strands of hair from getting into food items. Food handlers should also wear disposable gloves to keep pathogens on their fingers and hands from being transmitted to food.

Selecting Food

Just as important as the cleanliness of the store and the food handlers is the quality of the food that is purchased. Even when supermarket personnel are diligent about providing the safest food

Supermarket employees who are well trained in hygienic food-handling practices are a key to preventing food poisoning.

for their clients, infected food can get into the food supply. By taking a number of steps, consumers can ensure the quality of the food they purchase. One important step is checking use-by dates on packaged meats, poultry, dairy products, and refrigerated foods. This date indicates when the food loses its quality. After this date the food may spoil. When this happens bacteria multiplies rapidly and mold forms.

Another important stamp on meat and poultry indicates that the product has been inspected and approved by the USDA. This guarantees that safe food handling practices have been followed in the processing of the product.

Food Packaging

The use-by date and USDA stamp are not the only things that shoppers need to be aware of in order to avoid food poisoning. How meats and poultry are packaged is also important. If they are not packaged properly, cross-contamination, a process in which pathogens from infected food are unintentionally transferred to uninfected food, can occur.

Meat and poultry are usually placed on a foam tray and covered with plastic wrap. If the plastic wrap is not attached tightly, contaminated juices can leak out and get on the shopper's hands. As the consumer touches other foods, those too become infected. Food science and nutrition educator, Cynthia J. Speegle explains: "We pick up some chicken, and juices leak out of the corner of the package. Then we go and look at squash and tomatoes. We handle the squash and tomatoes and cross-contamination occurs."[32]

Leaky meat packages can also contaminate the inside of a shopping cart and the conveyor belt at the checkout counter, once again causing cross-contamination when food items touch these surfaces. Laura Day, the secretary of Safe Tables Our Priority, or S.T.O.P., an organization that seeks to prevent food poisoning, explains that meat and poultry should be securely wrapped because: "One cell of E. coli is enough to make someone violently ill, possibly kill them. A dripping package can contaminate a shopper's produce, the cart where children often sit, the conveyor belt at the checkout. When we get it home, what

A Cautious Consumer Speaks

In Spoiled, *food poisoning expert Nicols Fox explains the importance of being alert when purchasing food.*

"Becoming a discerning food buyer is a process of training or retraining the senses as well as a matter of priority. Our eyes filter constantly, choosing only those things we want or need to see. . . . When we readjust our eyes, we see things we never saw before.

I stand before the girl at the dairy bar, and as I decide what drink to have I watch her rub the rim of the paper cup she holds around her opposite palm. Then, incredibly, she unconsciously extends her hand into the cup, turning it as she does. She tosses it away with annoyance when I mention it. My eyes now see what I never saw before—the many violations of basic food-safety rules that go on around us daily. My local grocery store has put cooked (ready-to-eat) shrimp on the ice next to the raw shrimp that undoubtedly carry pathogens. Another local store places packages of cut vegetables (presumably to inspire stir-frying) in the meat counter next to fresh beef and chicken—a practice that could easily spread contamination. Chicken drips its watery, pathogen-laden trail down the conveyor belt at the check-out counter, and I watch shoppers put fresh vegetables on the same belt. My farmstand wants to put fresh bread into a recycled bag that contained who knows what and doesn't understand my objection. My favorite restaurant is totally open. I can watch pizza being built, watch how the vegetables are cut up. That sort of openness inspires confidence."

Storing foods, especially meats, in airtight packages at cold temperatures reduces the risk of contamination by foodborne pathogens.

will it matter if we cook our ground beef thoroughly if E. coli has already dripped onto the lettuce that will be used in salad?"[33]

One should also pay attention to the shape of canned goods. *Clostridium botulinum* can cause cans to become misshapen. Therefore, in order to avoid this toxin, such cans should be avoided. Speegle explains: "We've all come home from the store with cans that are slightly dented. That's not a concern. But we do need to look for cans with bulging convex lids. It may be an indication of the botulism organism."[34]

Food Storage

Once food has been selected and purchased, it is important that meat, fish, poultry, frozen foods, and dairy products be kept cool, especially in hot weather. In fact, food science experts say that these food items should always be kept at a temperature of 40 degrees Fahrenheit or less. This temperature does not kill harmful bacteria but causes the pathogens to become dormant and harmless. At temperatures between 50 degrees and 145 degrees Fahrenheit bacteria quickly multiply. Therefore, it is important that these foods are refrigerated as soon as possible. For this reason, some people transport cold foods in an ice chest that they keep in their vehicle. Transporting the food in the trunk of the vehicle, on the other hand, is risky. Air does not circulate well in a closed trunk, so the trunk heats up quickly in warm weather. "Food temperature is a big concern," Speegle explains.

"We need to keep hot food hot, and cold food cold. Say you buy a steak or a chicken and you throw it in the trunk of your car. Then you drive around in El Paso, Texas, in July when it's one hundred degrees. A few hours later you get home. The real concern is that the high temperature in your car allows bacteria to thrive. By the time you get that steak or chicken home it will be completely infected."[35]

Once an individual gets the food home, storing the food at the proper temperature still remains a concern. A safe temperature for a refrigerator is a maximum of forty degrees. And certain foods like dairy products and eggs need to be placed in the coolest part of the refrigerator in order to maintain a safe temperature. Consequently, food safety experts do not advise that consumers store these items on the door of the refrigerator, since it does not get as cold as the inside shelves.

Experts say that frozen food should be kept in freezers that are set at a maximum of zero degrees Fahrenheit. To prevent the growth of pathogens, even when these foods are being thawed they should be kept in the refrigerator. Leaving frozen food to thaw on a countertop provides an ideal environment for pathogens to multiply. While thawing, although the inside of the food item may still be frozen, the outside will not stay cold enough to prevent the growth of bacteria.

Food Preparation and Handling

Careful preparation and handling of food is also vital in preventing food poisoning. Before preparing a meal, people who want to avoid food poisoning wash their hands thoroughly with hot water and soap for at least twenty seconds. This procedure destroys or at least reduces any harmful pathogens on their hands. Dan Henroid, a food safety specialist at Iowa State University in Ames explains: "When I wash my hands, I'm going to use soap and warm water. I'm going to rub my hands for twenty seconds, use a single-service towel and not touch the faucet handle with my clean hands. Some one else might run their hands under cold water for a few seconds, and then use the dishtowel next to the sink."[36] The latter procedure will not eliminate pathogens.

For the same reason, while preparing food careful cooks wash their hands after any activity that might expose them to contaminants, such as sneezing, blowing their nose, changing diapers, going to the toilet, or handling garbage. Students in high school and college food science classes, for example, must wash their hands with antibacterial soap as soon as they enter the food lab, as well as each time they reenter the laboratory after leaving the room. Similarly, McDonald's employees are required to wash their hands with a disinfectant every thirty minutes.

Hand washing is so important that many experts estimate that half of all food poisoning cases in the United States are caused by dirty hands. In fact, a 2001 outbreak caused by the Norwalk virus, affecting three hundred people in Snellville, Georgia, was attributed to a cake decorator who failed to wash her hands thoroughly.

Hand washing is also important in preventing cross contamination, which can easily happen if a cook handles raw meat, seafood, or poultry, and then fails to wash his or her hands before handling fruits and vegetables. Utensils such as spatulas and cutting boards that have been in contact with raw meats, seafood, and poultry and then come in contact with produce or cooked foods can also cause cross-contamination. For example, many people use the same spatula to put raw burgers onto a grill and then to transfer the cooked burgers onto a plate. The spatula picks up pathogens from the raw meat and then transmits them to the cooked food. Nicols Fox describes such a case:

> Two teenagers came in after school and prepared hamburger patties, one after the other. . . . The first boy cooked his burger. Then the second one placed a raw burger in a pan with a cake turner [in place of a spatula] as the first boy's burger was ready to be taken from the heat. The first boy then used the cake turner to pick up his cooked hamburger. He was the boy who became ill, presumably from contamination transferred to the cooked burger from the raw burger.[37]

Washing one's hands with soap and hot water before handling foods or food-preparation tools helps to prevent the transmission of germs.

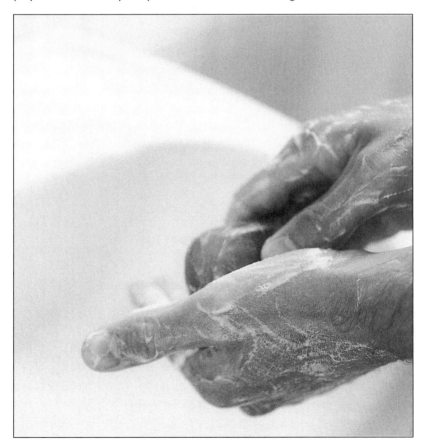

The same thing occurs when people use the same cutting board for cutting up raw meat and produce. Therefore, experts advise cooks to thoroughly wash these tools each time they are used or to have more than one of each tool available. Cynthia J. Speegle explains that in the food science laboratory that she supervises,

> Meals are prepared using two or more different cutting boards, one for fruits and vegetables and one for meats. I tell my students that if they only have one cutting board, they should always cut their fruits and vegetables first, not their chicken since it's more likely to be infected and cause cross-contamination. Then they need to wash the cutting board with dish soap and one teaspoon of bleach before cutting another food on it.[38]

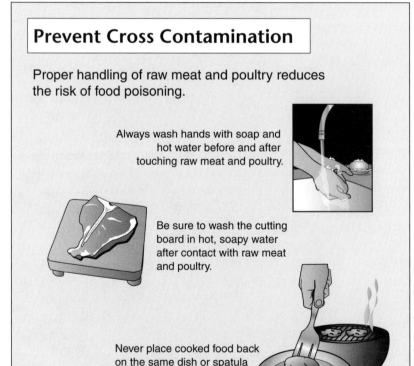

Prevent Cross Contamination

Proper handling of raw meat and poultry reduces the risk of food poisoning.

Always wash hands with soap and hot water before and after touching raw meat and poultry.

Be sure to wash the cutting board in hot, soapy water after contact with raw meat and poultry.

Never place cooked food back on the same dish or spatula that touched the raw food.

Source: Partnership for Food Safety Education.

For the same reason, kitchen counters and food preparation tables should be cleaned often with an antibacterial cleanser. These surfaces can harbor pathogens, which can easily be transferred to a cook's hands or to uninfected food. Indeed, a 2002 outbreak of *Campylobacter* food poisoning that affected sixty-five inmates in a Washington State penitentiary was linked to a contaminated food preparation table.

Using a sponge to clean those surfaces, however, is a bad idea. *Salmonella* bacteria thrive in a sponge's moist holes. Food poisoning experts Elizabeth Scott and Paul Sockett explain: "Sponges and dishcloths can provide the perfect living conditions for kitchen germs because they are moist and warm and often trap bits of food particles. More than 1 billion germs can grow in a sponge in twenty four hours of use."[39]

Cooking Safety

Fruits and vegetables with edible skin also need to be washed thoroughly in order to eliminate pathogens and microscopic bits of fertilizer, soil, and insects. Scrubbing these fruits with a scrub brush after the fruits have been washed is an additional step that helps eliminate pathogens. Nicols Fox cautions: "Remember you never buy the first apple you pick up. Many other people have touched the fruits and vegetables you purchase, not only as they were picked or packed, but in the open bins of the grocery store."[40]

Moreover, many food experts suggest that people wash the outside of all fruits, not just those with edible skin, so that when these fruits are cut the knife will not carry pathogens from the skin onto the interior surface of the fruit. Indeed, a number of outbreaks of *Salmonella* food poisoning have been traced to unwashed cantaloupe skin. New Mexico State University food and nutrition specialist, Martha Archuleta explains: "Cantaloupe can become contaminated with salmonella after contact with fecal matter in the field. . . . The important thing is to wash cantaloupe immediately before you plan to eat it. Just use cold water and a scrub brush. That way when you slice into the cantaloupe you don't drag the bacteria that was on the outside into the meat of the cantaloupe."[41]

Further precautions should be taken when cooks prepare meats, poultry, and eggs. In general these food items harbor pathogens when they are raw. However, when these foods are fully cooked, most pathogens are destroyed and the risk of food

Are Prewashed Salads Safe?

Bagged, prewashed salad greens are sold everywhere. Since the greens are prewashed many consumers do not rewash the greens. Is this practice safe? Nicols Fox does not think so. This is what she says in Spoiled:

"One of the fastest developing trends in the fresh produce industry is the packaged salad, sometimes containing a variety of attractive fresh greens and often even a packet of dressing and croutons. These packages are marked "pre-washed" or "triple-washed," labeling that encourages use without further washing. With their attractive packaging, these salad packages carry the reassuring veneer of technology. Not long ago I watched with growing unease as a friend of mine prepared a salad in my home from greens she had brought with her. She took the . . . lettuce from the open-topped plastic bag and tore it into the bowl without even a cursory washing. We all survived.

This same trusting friend of mine was watching not long ago as I filled a pan with water and emptied into it a "triple-washed" package of mixed exotic greens. This time my caution paid off visibly. We were both startled to see a truly significant amount of black soil at the bottom of the pan when I fished the greens out. When I called the distributor to ask whether the salad was, in fact, ready to eat, he replied that he would wash the salad before serving."

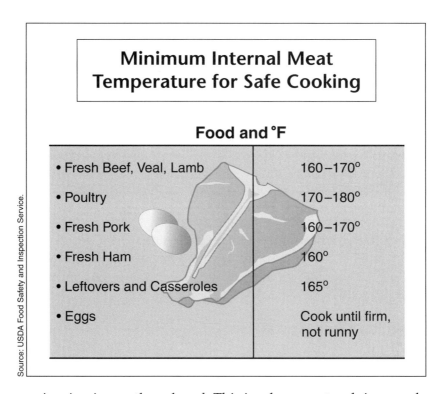

Minimum Internal Meat Temperature for Safe Cooking

Food and °F

Food	°F
• Fresh Beef, Veal, Lamb	160–170°
• Poultry	170–180°
• Fresh Pork	160–170°
• Fresh Ham	160°
• Leftovers and Casseroles	165°
• Eggs	Cook until firm, not runny

poisoning is greatly reduced. This is why experts advise people never to eat raw meat or eggs. Indeed, even rare meats and soft-boiled or runny eggs pose a risk. Therefore, to ensure that pathogens have been destroyed, all meats and poultry should be well-done, and egg yolks should be hard. To guarantee that meats are well-done, their internal temperature can be monitored. This is done by inserting a meat thermometer into the product. The internal temperature should be at least 160 degrees. This is the lowest temperature at which pathogens are destroyed. In addition, when cooks cut into meats and poultry the internal juices should be clear. If they are pink or red, this is an indication that the food is not sufficiently cooked and pathogens have not been destroyed. Cooking meat and poultry thoroughly is so effective in destroying pathogens that many food science experts say it is the number one way to prevent food poisoning.

Once food is thoroughly cooked it is important not to leave it sitting out before it is served, since bacteria quickly multiply at room temperature. Morton Satin describes an outbreak that was caused in this fashion:

At a New Mexico country club buffet, on March 30, 1986, a large number of people came down with . . . diarrhea, nausea, painful abdominal cramps, vomiting, fever, and bloody stools. . . . When the food handling procedures were reviewed, it turned out that the turkey had cooled for three hours at room temperature after cooking—plenty of time for staphylococcal toxins to develop to poisonous levels.[42]

For the same reason, once diners have finished eating, leftovers must be put into the refrigerator quickly. And, to prevent infection when reheating leftovers, they too need to be heated to at least 160 degrees, while reheated soups and sauces should be brought to a rolling boil.

Food Safety in Restaurants

Most of the food safety problems that occur in homes also occur in restaurants. Therefore, food preparers and handlers in restaurants must take the same precautions that individuals do at home in order to prevent food poisoning. Indeed, when people eat in restaurants they depend on the restaurant staff to practice good food safety methods. However, there are steps that individuals can take to protect themselves when eating out. As with food stores, restaurants that are conscientious about food safety generally look and smell clean. Experts agree that if a restaurant does not look fresh and clean, then the kitchen is probably not clean either. Nicols Fox explains:

> If you know nothing else about a restaurant, dirty windows, weeds growing in cracks in the sidewalk, garbage strewn around the back entrance and a messy or grimy look to the interior will tell you the cleanliness is not a high priority. One public health official uses the cleanliness of the bathroom as her clue to the restaurant's standards. An eating establishment that isn't careful to keep clean what its patrons can see, won't be careful about what patrons can't see.[43]

Cleanliness means that not only the interior and exterior of the restaurant are clean but also the tabletops, tablecloths, cutlery, plates, and glasses. If any of these items are unclean, pathogens can be transmitted when customers come in contact with them. Therefore, a customer who is given a dirty glass, for example, would be wise to ask for another.

Careful Food Ordering

Once a restaurant is selected, many experts say that it is sensible to avoid ordering risky foods such as raw fish and seafood that often harbor parasitic worms. Indeed, the majority of food poisoning cases involving fish and seafood occur in Japan and Korea where raw fish is commonly eaten.

To help prevent contamination, many Japanese restaurants that serve raw fish in the form of sushi have a special light table in the kitchen. When raw fish is placed on the light table, worms can be seen by the naked eye. Infected fish is then discarded. Freezing fish for a week before the fish is defrosted and eaten raw also kills worms. Therefore, in order to lower the risk of infecting individuals who order raw fish, it is important that these practices are a part of the restaurant's sushi preparation.

Raw oysters are also dangerous. In fact, eating raw oysters is so unsafe that three states, California, Louisiana, and Florida, require that restaurants that serve them post a warning on their menus.

Salad bars and buffets are another area of concern. Foods on a salad bar or buffet may not be kept cold or warm enough, allowing bacteria to grow. Customers may also spread infection by touching items on the salad bar or buffet with their bare hands or sneezing or coughing on the food items. In addition, customers often cause cross-contamination by switching utensils that are provided for individual items on a buffet. Speegle explains: "It's an uncontrollable environment. You have sneezing, unwashed hands, food sitting out. There are unlimited possibilities of contaminants coming in contact with the food. It is less than safe."[44]

Safety While Traveling

Individuals can take other precautions when traveling, especially in developing nations where sanitation systems may be ineffective and the drinking water unsafe. One way travelers to these nations can protect themselves is by getting vaccinated against hepatitis A before leaving home. In fact, the Centers for Disease Control strongly recommend that people who travel to developing nations get this vaccination.

Another precaution travelers can take is to avoid drinking tap water. Instead, they should drink bottled water. Cautious travelers also avoid ice for drinks and fruits and vegetables that may have been washed in local water. In many cases, the local water supply may be so contaminated that travelers are warned to use bottled water when they brush their teeth. Nicols Fox describes the case of her friend: "She was being careful on a trip to Central America but came down with a serious parasitic infection on her return. The only risk she could remember taking was brushing her teeth with tap water."[45]

Buying food from street vendors who often lack food safety training is also hazardous. Street vendors may not follow the same standards of cleanliness as restaurants. Food items may be

Eating from restaurant salad bars and buffets where food sits out for long periods puts diners at higher risk for food poisoning.

Street vendors in foreign countries like this woman in Laos often lack food-safety training and sell food that is at a high risk for contamination.

exposed to heat and insects for long periods of time until they are sold, conditions that invite infection. Outdoor buffets, which are popular at many resort hotels, pose a similar problem.

Local customs can also endanger travelers. In some restaurants in Indonesia, for instance, bowls of food are set out on tables and people eat from these bowls with their fingers. Diners are not charged by the bowl but rather by the amount of food that they consume. Therefore, when diners finish eating, food that remains in these communal bowls is topped off and placed on the next diner's table. It is not surprising that pathogens can easily be transmitted in this manner, and travelers are advised to avoid such local practices.

Clearly, whether individuals are traveling, shopping, or in their own home, there is no foolproof method of avoiding food poisoning. But when people are alert and take precautionary steps they can greatly reduce their risk of infection. The Food and Drug Administration's Center for Food Safety and Applied Nutrition research microbiologist, Donald H. Burr agrees. "Consumers," he says, "have a responsibility in food safety."[46]

Chapter 4

Protecting the Public

IT IS TRUE that taking precautionary measures can help individuals avoid food poisoning, but it cannot entirely stop outbreaks from occurring. In an effort to keep the public safe, the government and the food industry have taken a number of steps to protect the food supply and thus prevent widespread outbreaks. In fact, in 1997 former president Bill Clinton enacted a $43 million food safety initiative aimed at making food safer for all Americans.

At least twelve federal agencies, numerous state and local agencies, and the food industry are involved in this effort. Among these agencies are the U.S. Department of Agriculture, the Environmental Protection Agency, the Centers for Disease Control, the Department of Health and Human Services, the Department of Homeland Security, and the Food and Drug Administration. Their efforts involve tracing and responding to food poisoning outbreaks, inspecting and monitoring the food supply, educating the public, and preventing and planning a response to bioterrorism involving the nation's food.

Tracking Cases

In an effort to recognize the causes of food poisoning and gain a better understanding of how to prevent possible outbreaks, the Foodborne Disease Surveillance Network, or FoodNet was established in 1996. Just as its name implies, FoodNet is an active surveillance network of foodborne disease cases. Operating as a cooperative endeavor between the Centers for Disease Control, the Food Safety and Inspection Service of the USDA, the Food and Drug Administration, and state health departments, Food-Net's primary objective is to track food poisoning cases in which individuals seek medical care and to identify any patterns that may exist among those cases.

Before the establishment of FoodNet, many severe food poisoning cases were not reported. This is because the reporting of

A researcher with the U.S. Department of Agriculture examines a sample of food under a microscope for the presence of harmful bacteria.

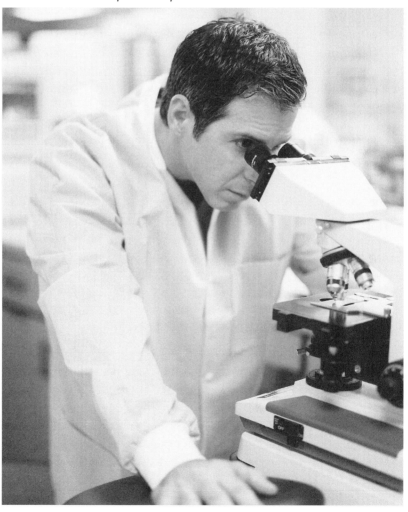

food poisoning cases depended on a complex chain of events. First, laboratories that identified food poisoning pathogens in stool cultures reported the occurrence to the local health department. The local agency then reported to the state health department, which in turn reported to the Centers for Disease Control. Each report required the completion of complex forms. Often cases went unreported because of a break in the chain.

FoodNet simplifies this process. FoodNet scientists work directly with 450 laboratories throughout the United States. Officials at these laboratories are contacted regularly by FoodNet investigators collecting information on confirmed cases of food poisoning. This eliminates the possibility of breaks in the chain.

What's more, because contacts and reports are done electronically, it allows information to be transmitted quickly and easily. Among the data that is reported is the location of the case, the age and gender of the victim, what food item caused infection, and the identity of the pathogen, if these last two items have been established. The information is entered into a database known as the Electronic Foodborne Outbreak Reporting System. The database is accessible to FoodNet officials and state and local health departments. In fact, food poisoning cases identified in laboratories that are not part of the FoodNet network can also be recorded directly onto the database. This helps FoodNet experts to keep track of the number of food poisoning cases occurring at any time, determine the yearly incidence of cases caused by specific pathogens, and identify specific trends that may be occurring.

Linking the Pathogen and the Source

Once this information is gathered, FoodNet investigators look for patterns among reported cases. The existence of a common pathogen and food source in a number of cases is an indication that a food poisoning outbreak is occurring.

It is not always easy to make this connection. That is why PulseNet, a branch of FoodNet, was established. By using DNA testing, profiles of bacteria strains were created by PulseNet scientists and stored on an electronic database. Using these profiles, scientists match the characteristics of the infecting bacterium with

State Laws
Keep Food Safe

In addition to federal regulations, individual states have passed laws to protect the public from contaminated food. One such law is a California law concerning oysters. The law prohibits oyster farmers from harvesting oysters in California's Tomales Bay for up to a week when it rains a half an inch or more. This is because during heavy rains runoff pollutes the bay with fecal matter from nearby dairy farms. As a result, pathogens are likely to get inside the oysters when algae is filtered through their shells. It takes at least a week for the pathogens to be filtered out of the oysters' systems. As a result of the law, California oyster farms have been closed for as many as one hundred days each year.

To a help prevent contamination from occurring, dairy farmers have been working to contain cow waste. They have construed storage ponds to hold manure and fences to contain runoff and keep cows from walking into creeks that drain into Tomales Bay. In fact, in 2000 oyster and dairy farmers, environmentalists, and government agencies formed an alliance known as the Tomales Bay Watershed Council with the goal of keeping Tomales Bay clean. In 2003 the council developed a plan to achieve this goal.

By working together these groups are hoping to keep fecal matter out of the bay, thus making eating oysters safer. In an Associated Press article, the owner of the Tomales Bay Oyster Company, Drew Alden, explains: "People are taking steps to address this issue. They are willing to look at the problems with a critical eye. Change will come slowly."

that of its strain. Once the strain is determined, PulseNet scientists use DNA fingerprints to further classify the bacterium and link it to its source.

Like individual fingerprints, pathogens that come from the same source have the same DNA profile or fingerprint. The fingerprint can be seen through a process known as pulsed field gel electrophoresis in which a conductive gel is smeared on samples of the pathogen. The pathogen is then placed in an electrical field and observed. Each individual pathogen alters the direction of the electrical field in a distinct manner. This is the pathogen's fingerprint. The *E. coli* O157:H7 that infects a batch of hamburger meat produced at a single source will have a unique fingerprint that matches exactly the fingerprint of the *E. coli* O157:H7 found in food samples and stool samples wherever that infected hamburger was distributed. However, other cases of *E.coli* O157:H7, which are transmitted from a different source, have a different fingerprint.

After scientists at PulseNet laboratories have identified and fingerprinted a pathogen, the fingerprint and specifics about the case it is related to are published on the Electronic Food-borne Outbreak Report System. This permits investigators and scientists to rapidly compare bacteria fingerprints and determine whether an outbreak from a common source is occurring even if the victims are geographically far apart. This is important because with the global distribution of food, outbreaks from a single source can occur in multiple states or in different countries. Since the information is available electronically, the determination is made in a few hours rather than in weeks. Such prompt recognition of an outbreak lets experts quickly warn distributors about the contaminated food before an epidemic occurs.

Recalling Food

Once PulseNet scientists identify the source of infection, FoodNet officials notify the manufacturer of the product as well as food outlets in which it is sold. As a result, merchants remove the product before it can cause further problems and the manufacturer issues a recall of the item.

The public is made aware of a food recall through a press release, which includes a description of the food, any identifying codes, the name of the producer, distribution information, and the reason for the recall. Consumers are urged to return the product to the place it was purchased. There, the consumer is reimbursed for the cost of the item. One such recall in July 2002 involved 19 million pounds of hamburger meat. At the time of the recall sixteen people in Colorado had contracted *E. coli* poisoning, which was linked to the meat. The prompt recall protected countless other individuals.

Once investigators have determined a geographic pattern of food poisoning, doctors and health agencies throughout the affected area are alerted to the problem and the identity of the infecting pathogen. This allows health care professionals to immediately prescribe the most effective treatment for patients. In this manner, FoodNet and PulseNet professionals deter large-scale food poisoning outbreaks before they occur and ensure that food poisoning victims receive proper care.

HACCP and Food Monitoring

Another way the government and the food industry are protecting the public is through the Hazardous Analysis and Critical Control Points system (HACCP). HACCP is a total quality control system that monitors food from the farm to the time it reaches the consumer. In HACCP, the food industry with the assistance of Food and Drug Administration inspectors, analyze and monitor the production of food with the goal of determining when and where things could possibly go wrong that could lead to the contamination of the final product. When weak points in the food production process are identified, changes are made to rectify the problem and eliminate the chance of contamination occurring. HACCP shifts the emphasis from identifying contaminated foods to preventing contamination from occurring. It has been mandatory since 2000.

As a result of HACCP, there have been a number of positive changes in the food industry. For example, HACCP identified the problem of chickens becoming contaminated with bacteria from

Farm-to-Table Continuum

HACCP ensures quality control from production to consumption and aims to prevent food contamination.

Farming

Eggs and Dairy

Imports

Shipping

Processing

MARKET

Consumer

Source: www.nal.usda.gov/fsrio-ppd/fola07i.htm.

their digestive tracts during slaughter. As a result, chickens are now routinely sprayed inside and out with a disinfectant right after they are slaughtered. Fish processing has also improved because, since the inception of HACCP, fish processors require proof that fish has been placed on ice from the time it is caught until the time it reaches the processing plant. If this proof is not available, plants refuse to purchase the fish. Beef processing methods, too, have become safer as a result of HACCP. In fact, because of HACCP, beef processing plants are using a high-temperature steam vacuum system on beef carcasses. The system uses steam and a vacuum-like instrument to remove and destroy contaminants on meat. As an extra precaution, after this process is completed the beef is tested for *E.coli.* Contaminated beef is immediately destroyed.

Therefore, it is not surprising that the Centers for Disease Control and the food industry agree that HACCP has improved food safety. James Hodges, the president of the American Meat Institute, a national meatpackers trade organization, explains: "Our slaughter facilities are approaching a better-than-hospital sanitation standard."[47]

Moreover, in an effort to further protect the public some companies have taken HACCP a step further. In addition to conducting required HACCP monitoring, these companies hire independent food safety experts to monitor and rate their facilities based on food safety and cleanliness. The IGA supermarket chain, for example, routinely follows this procedure. "During each supermarket review," an IGA press release explains, "approximately 1,200 areas of operations are checked including product selection, store appearance, use of technology, employee uniforms and others."[48]

Making Farming Safer

In addition to the HACCP system and the hiring of independent food safety consultants, the food industry is taking other steps to keep the food supply safe. Among these are changing to farming methods that keep animals from becoming infected with food poisoning pathogens. These include changing the animal feed.

In the past, cattle were given supplemental feed that contained, among other things, ground-up chicken feces. Chicken feces are a good source of nitrogen, which cattle convert to protein. However, because chicken feces can harbor *Salmonella* and other pathogens, which may be transmitted to cattle via the feed and then to humans who eat the cattle, this feeding practice was stopped in 2004. New Mexico Farm and Livestock Bureau president Michael White explains: "There is nothing we [farmers and ranchers] take more seriously than the health of our families, our animals, and the consumers of this nation. . . . Our focus . . . [is] growing and maintaining the safest food supply in the world."[49]

Food Inspections

As partners with farmers, ranchers, and processors and distributors of food, U.S. Department of Agriculture agents regularly inspect the nation's food supply. In order to prevent contaminated food items from reaching consumers, the Food Safety and Inspection Service of the USDA has more than seventy-six hundred food safety inspectors working in sixty-five hundred privately owned slaughtering and processing plants throughout the United States. The inspectors' job is to examine the animals before and after slaughter in order to prevent unhealthy animals from reaching consumers. In a typical year, food safety inspectors inspect over 8 billion pounds of poultry, 140 million head of livestock, and 4.5 billion eggs. Inspectors also monitor and inspect any product that contains meat or poultry such as frozen dinners, pizzas, meat pies, and soup, as well as processed meat and poultry like bologna, pepperoni, salami, hot dogs, ham, bacon, and sausage. As part of inspection procedures, the inspector tests processed meat and poultry for the presence of *E.coli, Salmonella*, and *Listeria*. In addition, inspectors monitor the plant's food safety standards, processing procedures, product contents, and packaging and labeling.

Inspecting Supermarkets and Restaurants

Supermarkets and restaurants, too, are carefully monitored. Local health department inspectors routinely check these facilities for cleanliness and hygienic food safety practices. Depending on the municipality, these inspections occur every 60 to 120 days and involve a long list of items. For instance, in a typical restaurant inspection the temperatures of all prepared food, both hot and cold, are checked. The temperatures of the refrigerators and freezers are also examined, and if the temperature in a refrigerator is above forty degrees, the inspector orders that all the food in the refrigerator be discarded. The serving line, where standing food is kept until waiters pick it up, is also monitored, as are canned goods. If cans are misshapen or food on the serving line is not hot or cold enough, these items too must be discarded.

This food-processing worker inspects seafood for parasites. Careful inspection can prevent foodborne diseases from spreading.

These government food inspectors check food safety practices in a fast-food restaurant before giving the restaurant a food safety rating.

Inspectors also check for any signs of insects or rodents. This includes not just live animals but also dead animals and insect trails. Even cracks in the walls are checked for insects and dirt. And, to detect the presence of mice, inspectors use a special black light that illuminates mouse urine, which is invisible to the naked eye.

These are not the only ways inspectors check for cleanliness. Inspectors check that all material in the kitchen is cleaned properly. They make sure cloths that are used to clean restaurant tables are kept in a sanitizing solution. They check the fryers, vent hoods, and filters for cleanliness. Even bathrooms and air-conditioning units are examined. These too must be clean and well maintained.

The water supply is another area of inspection. Inspectors make sure that the water supply is fresh and the temperature is proper for washing hands and dishes. Indeed, inspectors check about eighty different items. Then the restaurant or supermarket is given a score from zero to one hundred. Different items on the checklist carry a different weight. Some items such as unsafe food temperatures or impure water are considered critical violations and carry more weight than other items. A score of sixty or less is considered unsatisfactory. A restaurant may receive such a rating if it has four or more critical violations. When a restaurant is rated unsatisfactory and the inspector thinks that the violations pose an imminent health hazard, the restaurant is closed down immediately. If the violations are not as risky, the inspector gives the restaurant management a maximum of ten days to rectify the problems. Then the inspector comes back to reinspect. At this point the restaurant will get a new rating or be closed down.

On the other hand, to receive a passing score and get an approved rating, a restaurant can have no more than three critical violations. The ratings are published in newspapers and on the Internet. In addition, many municipalities require restaurants to post their ratings in their lobbies for customers to see. Indeed, most restaurant personnel are proud to do this. Marty, a former restaurant owner, explains: "The restaurant owner and the food inspector have a common purpose. It's a matter of trust. You both work hard to provide the public with good, safe food."[50]

Preventing Bioterrorism

Besides protecting the public from normal food poisoning outbreaks, since the September 11, 2001, terrorist attacks, federal, state, and local government agencies have taken steps to protect the public from the possibility of terrorists contaminating the nation's food or water supply. Officials agree that terrorists might try to cripple the country's economy and hurt American citizens by planting disease agents in imported food products or anywhere along the food distribution chain. Terrorists might also try to contaminate drinking water, infect farm animals with food poisoning pathogens, or infect plants such as corn or wheat with a fast-acting fungus that can destroy the crop.

To counter these threats, in 2004 President George W. Bush ordered the Department of Homeland Security, the Environmental Protection Agency, the Food and Drug Administration, the USDA, the CIA, the U.S. Customs Service, and the Department of Health and Human Services to work together to develop and implement new procedures to protect the nation's food supply. In ordering this plan, the president said: "We should provide the best protection possible against a successful attack on the United States agriculture and food system, which could have catastrophic health and economic effects."[51]

Under the plan the government agencies are working together to look for weak spots in agriculture and food distribution and develop ways to repair them. This includes increased inspection and screening of all food entering the United States. One area of concern is imported gum arabic plants, which are widely used as food additives. These are imported from Africa and the Middle East, areas of the world that government officials suspect have close ties to terrorist organizations that want to harm the United States. According to Michael Doyle, the director of the Center for Food Safety at the University of Georgia, "Terrorists could lace such imports with not only botulism toxin, but also other pathogens, including E. coli O157:H7, salmonella, . . . and hepatitis."[52]

In order to counter the threat to gum arabic plants and other food imports, USDA and U.S. Customs Service inspectors are stationed at ports of entry, docks, loading areas, and refrigeration and storage units throughout the country, where they monitor many imported food items. In addition, under the new plan any companies exporting food to the United States must notify the Food and Drug Administration about when and where the product is entering the country. Products or exporters that are deemed suspicious are met at the port of entry by special investigators who carefully inspect the product before it can be distributed to the public.

Another part of the protection system is the development of a plan to contain any outbreaks of plant or animal disease before contaminants can reach the public. This plan includes a way to stabilize the food supply and the economy if such an attack ever does occur. As part of the plan, the food industry is required to come up with procedures to protect itself. To assist, the Agriculture Department is developing the National Veterinary Stockpile of medications, which will be used to respond to animal disease outbreaks within twenty-four hours.

In addition, the nation's water utilities have developed a plan of preparedness in the event of an attack on the nation's water supply. At the same time, the Department of Homeland Security is conducting an assessment of different water systems with the intent of fixing vulnerable systems.

In an article on MSNBC, USDA director of homeland security Jeremy Stump describes the steps the government is taking to protect Americans: "It's from farm to fork. It's a protective shield around a whole sector."[53]

Educating the Public

Even with so many protective measures in place, government and food industry officials agree that without the cooperation of the public, food poisoning outbreaks cannot be prevented. Experts say that the more people know about food poisoning, the more likely they are to practice food safety.

One way the USDA is getting the word out is through the Food Safety Mobile. The Food Safety Mobile is manned by USDA food safety experts and decorated with colorful graphics depicting food safety rules. The vehicle travels throughout the United States to state fairs, schools, universities, supermarkets, and senior centers in an effort to educate the public on safe food handling and

Veterinarians in Indonesia vaccinate chickens against bird flu. Agencies worldwide try to maintain adequate supplies of vaccines in the event of animal disease outbreaks.

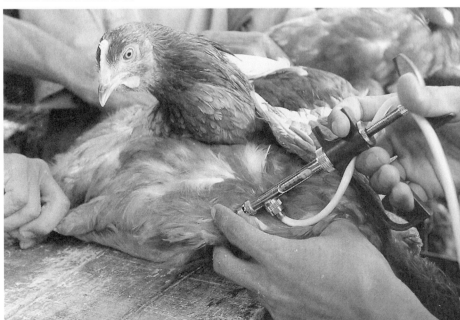

preparation. At each stop food safety experts demonstrate safe food handling techniques and answer questions. "Nothing teaches people quicker than seeing safe food handling in action," says USDA undersecretary for food safety, Elsa Murano. "When we show them how to cook hamburgers safely—how to use a food thermometer, how to clean their hands—then they have a whole new understanding of the actions they need to take."[54]

The USDA Fight BAC! program teaches students about food safety.

Another step the government and local school districts are taking is the implementation of a special hands-on food safety curriculum known as Fight BAC! Through Fight BAC! students in kindergarten through high school are instructed in the importance of food safety as part of the science curriculum. In the lower grades young learners are taught important steps of food safety such as proper hand washing, which they practice. Older students engage in science experiments that demonstrate important food safety concepts such as the temperature in which bacteria grow. Students, teachers, and food scientists agree that the program is quite effective. Food science educator Cynthia J. Speegle explains: "I know that it absolutely works. Starting the program early and making it a constant portion of the curriculum is just what is needed to keep us all well."[55]

Indeed, between education programs and the joint actions of the food industry and the government, numerous steps are being taken to keep consumers safe. Murano explains: "The cumulative effect of these initiatives is safer food and a healthier nation."[56]

Chapter 5

What the Future Holds

DESPITE THE STEPS individuals, the government, and the food industry are taking to prevent food poisoning, the threat of food becoming contaminated still exists. What makes matters worse is the emergence of a number of dangerous new pathogens that are more potent than older pathogens and, in many cases, are immune to antibiotics. Scientists are working hard to keep these pathogens, as well as older pathogens, out of the food supply. To accomplish this goal scientists are investigating new ways to keep food safe.

Emerging Pathogens

In order to ensure their survival, microorganisms mutate. In so doing they adapt to changes in the environment, gain the ability to infect new hosts, and develop immunity to medications that can destroy them. In fact, each time bacteria and viruses reproduce, their genes have the potential to randomly mutate. And since thousands of bacteria and viruses are produced every few minutes, chances are that many of the newly emerging mutated pathogens are stronger and better able to survive than those from which they were derived.

Indeed, in the last twenty-five years a host of new microorganisms and mutated strains of common food poisoning pathogens have emerged. These include *E. coli* O157:H7, *Listeria*, the Norwalk virus, *Campylobacter*, and a number of new strains of *Salmonella*, among others. According to food poisoning expert Nicols Fox, these varieties of pathogens were unknown as recently as the 1980s. Not only have these pathogens only recently

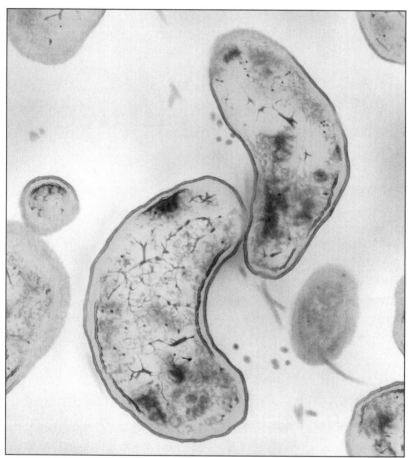

Campylobacter jejuni *is one of several mutated strains of food-poisoning pathogens to have emerged in the last twenty-five years.*

emerged, they have become the chief cause of current food poisoning cases. For example, the most common causes of food poisoning in the United States in the 1960s were the *Staphylococcus* and *Clostridium* bacteria. Today, although these pathogens still play a role, most food poisoning cases are linked to *Campylobacter*, *E. coli* O157:H7, and *Salmonella*. Making matters worse, infection with emerging pathogens is more likely to cause complications, such as HUS, than are infections caused by older pathogens. One reason is that just as microorganisms adapt in order to survive, so too does the human body. Therefore, when people are persistently exposed to a pathogen, over time they may develop immunity to that pathogen. Because of this the pathogen may not affect some people at all or, if it does, the illness usually will be mild. No such immunity exists when a new pathogen is involved. This explains why many people in developing nations who have been drinking contaminated tap water all their lives do not become ill, while tourists almost always become seriously ill after a brief exposure to the same water.

Antibiotic Resistance

Complicating matters, many emerging pathogens have developed antibiotic resistance. This means that unlike older bacteria, which could easily be destroyed with antibiotic treatment, many newly emerging bacteria are unharmed by antibiotics. This makes them less controllable and more dangerous.

There are a number of reasons why this happened. One reason is the widespread use of antibiotics in rearing animals. Because of factory farming methods in which animals are raised in close quarters, infectious diseases can spread rapidly. This has led to an increased use of antibiotics to combat infection. In fact, many farmers routinely dose healthy animals with antibiotics as a precautionary measure. In addition, because adding low levels of antibiotics to an animal's feed enhances the animal's growth, since the 1950s antibiotics have been added to the feed of poultry, cattle, and pigs. According to food expert Morton Satin, 25 million pounds of antibiotics are used in the United States each year as a standard component of animal feed. This is about half the antibiotics produced in the United States in a year.

Problems arise because the more an animal is exposed to an antibiotic, the more likely bacteria in the animal's body will develop ways to resist the effects of the drug. Once a bacterium mutates and develops antibiotic resistance, when the bacterium reproduces it passes on the resistance to its offspring. Complicating matters further, different species of bacteria regularly exchange bits of DNA with each other in a process known as plasmid transfer. This allows one type of bacteria that has developed antibiotic resistance to pass this property on to a different type of bacteria. It also allows bacteria that are resistant to one particular antibiotic like tetracycline, for example, to pass this resistance to another bacteria that may be resistant to a different antibiotic, such as ampicillin. After plasmid transfer, both bacteria are resistant to tetracycline and ampicillin. Eventually, some bacteria become multiresistant to so many types of antibiotics that they become seemingly indestructible. This is why *Salmonella typhimurium* DT104, an emerging strain of *Salmonella* immune to a wide range of antibiotics, is dubbed a "superbug." When such bacteria infect humans, traditional antibiotic treatment, which formerly cured a similar infection, has no effect.

Farm animals are routinely given antibiotics to prevent the spread of infection. Such overuse of antibiotics is one cause of mutated bacteria that resist the drugs.

Prions, a Deadly Emerging Pathogen

Another emerging pathogen that is causing concern among food scientists is the prion, which was discovered in 1995 by American scientist, Stanley Prusiner. Although not technically a microorganism, prions are mutated proteins that cause the bovine and human form of mad cow disease. Both are foodborne diseases with deadly consequences.

Mad cow disease first appeared in Great Britain in 1985. In the ensuing decade, the disease affected more than 180,000 cattle there. It was followed by over one hundred human cases, the first one occurring in 1993.

Cows contract mad cow disease when they eat feed infected with prions. Then, if a person eats meat from an infected cow, prions can be transmitted through the meat. As a result, the individual may develop the human form of mad cow disease.

Unlike most food poisoning pathogens, prions do not target the digestive tract. Instead, prions attack the brain, which makes them very dangerous. Indeed, once victims become infected with prions, their brains are gradually destroyed. Prions do this by transforming normal proteins in an individual's brain into prions. In the process, brain cells are killed. As a result, victims experience memory loss, hallucinations, and eventually lose their ability to think or recognize their friends and family. They lose their ability to walk, talk, or perform basic actions like swallowing. As a result, the human form of mad cow disease is invariably fatal. And, although scientists are actively seeking an agent that can kill prions, so far they have been unable to discover anything that can destroy these lethal pathogens.

A 1983 outbreak of *Salmonella* food poisoning in Minnesota shows how dangerous antibiotic-resistant pathogens can be. In this outbreak ten people ate hamburgers infected with *Salmonella* Newport, a strain of *Salmonella* which is resistant to at least nine antibiotics including tetracycline. The infected individuals were treated with a variety of antibiotics without success. Indeed, six of the victims were hospitalized and one died from the infection. When officials from the Centers for Disease Control investigated the outbreak, they found that the infected hamburgers came from a herd of cows that were regularly given tetracycline in their feed.

Morton Satin describes what happened to his daughter, Heather, when she became infected with another antibiotic-resistant strain of *Salmonella*:

> We took Heather to our family pediatrician who immediately asked us to bring her to the hospital. . . . She had a temperature of 105 degrees F that would not come down with the conventional antibiotic treatment. In order to keep her fever down, the pediatrician had her placed on a special ice-water mattress. It's impossible to forget the sight of this tiny little two-year-old lying prostrate on this freezing mattress, glistening with sweat. She remained this way for more than a week.[57]

Salmonella is not the only pathogen to develop antibiotic resistance. New strains of *Campylobacter* are also emerging. These pathogens have developed an immunity to ciprofloxacin, the drug most often administered to counter *Campylobacter* food poisoning. Scientists say that this resistance developed because enroflaxin, an antibiotic similar to ciprofloxacin, is commonly used in poultry and pig feed. Indeed the British government report that in 2002, 13 percent of all *Campylobacter* food poisoning cases in Great Britain were linked to antibiotic-resistant strains of *Campylobacter.*

What makes these emerging pathogens more worrisome is that, once they enter a person's body, they spread antibiotic immunity to other bacteria. When the individual becomes ill with

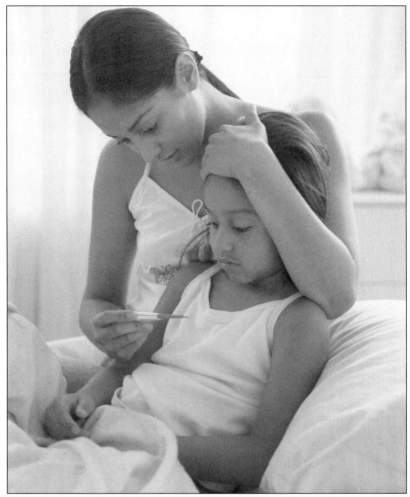

A mother checks her daughter's temperature. As more bacteria become antibiotic-resistant, illnesses such as tuberculosis and pneumonia may become difficult to contain.

any disease, including tuberculosis or pneumonia, antibiotic treatment is ineffective. World Health Organization director-general Gro Harlem Brundtland explains: "We currently have effective medicines to cure almost every major infectious disease. But we risk losing these valuable drugs and our opportunity to eventually control many infectious diseases because of increasing antimicrobial resistance [antibiotic-resistant bacteria]."[58]

A Test to Measure Antibiotic-Resistant Bacteria in Chicken

In 1997 and again in 2002, Consumer Reports *magazine tested over four hundred store-bought chickens for* Salmonella *and* Campylobacter *and analyzed the bacteria for antibiotic resistance. The results are reported in "Of Birds and Bacteria," an article that appeared in the January 2003 issue of* Consumer Reports.

"In the fall of 1997, almost three-fourths of the broilers that *Consumer Reports* bought in stores nationwide harbored salmonella or campylobacter—the bacteria most likely to give Americans food poisoning. Our new tests revealed contamination in about half of the chickens we analyzed, but there's a dark cloud within the silver lining. Many of the contaminated chickens harbored strains of salmonella and campylobacter that are resistant to antibiotics commonly used against those bugs, which can cause fever, diarrhea, and abdominal cramps. . . .

Campylobacter was present in 42 percent of the chickens, salmonella in 12 percent. Five percent of all chickens had both campylobacter and salmonella; 51 percent had neither . . . . Ninety percent of the campylobacter bacteria tested from our chicken and 34 percent of the salmonella showed resistance to one or more antibiotics. . . .

Our tests showed that if you are sickened by one of those chickens, two commonly used antibiotics—tetracycline, an older but still important drug used against germs from pneumonia to chlamydia, and erythromycin, an option for patients allergic to penicillin—may not help. In 66 percent of the campylobacter-contaminated chickens, the bacteria were resistant to tetracycline. In 20 percent, they were resistant to erythromycin.

Your chances of being cured by the usual doses of two fluoroquinolones, ciprofloxacin and ofloxacin, may also be limited. The latest figures from the FDA, reported in 2001, indicate that 11,477 Americans were infected in 1999 by fluoroquinolone-resistant campylobacter in chicken."

Making Food Safer with Biotechnology

To combat the threat of emerging pathogens as well as older pathogens, scientists are using biotechnology. Biotechnology involves using living organisms to modify a plant or animal. Such alterations make foods stay fresher longer, resist dangerous pathogens, and improve the nutritional value of a food. For example, in a process known as genetic engineering in which scientists manipulate hereditary information contained in DNA molecules, scientists have been able to slow down the ripening, softening, and rotting process of tomatoes. This was achieved by isolating the gene that causes tomatoes to soften. Scientists then converted the gene into a reverse image of itself and inserted it into tomato plants. The reversed gene, named FlavrSavr, slowed

A scientist injects FlavrSavr, a reversed tomato gene, into a tomato to prevent it from ripening too quickly.

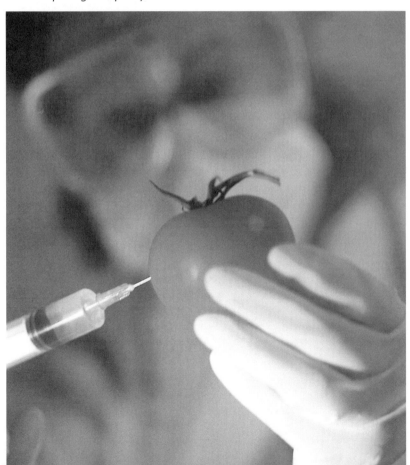

down the original ripening gene. This modification keeps tomatoes fresher longer, thereby protecting the public from dangerous bacteria, mold, and toxins that form as a tomato rots.

FlavrSavr tomatoes were introduced in 1994 in California supermarkets, but problems followed. For reasons scientists do not understand, some plants switched off the FlavrSavr gene and ripened normally. This made it impossible to produce enough FlavrSavr tomatoes to meet the demand for the product. Therefore, in 1996 the tomatoes were removed from the market. In the meantime, scientists are continuing to investigate what went wrong in hopes of rectifying the problem. In addition, scientists are working on developing a similar gene that would slow down the ripening, softening, and rotting process in strawberries, bananas, bell peppers, and melons.

Manufacturing Antibodies

Creating the FlavrSavr gene is not the only way that scientists are using biotechnology to prevent food poisoning. Some scientists are examining antibodies in hopes of duplicating them. When pathogens enter an animal or person's digestive system, antibodies locate, attack, and destroy them. Scientists want to duplicate antibodies in laboratories. Once this is done, they plan to use the antibodies to detect pathogens in food. This would help keep contaminated food from reaching consumers.

In fact, scientists Harold Craighead and Carl Batt of Cornell University in Ithaca, New York, have developed a handheld sensor, similar to a supermarket UPC bar-code wand, that detects *E. coli* O157:H7. The sensor contains *E. coli* O157:H7 antibodies that are stamped onto a sticky silicon chip. When the device is passed over a product containing *E. coli* O157:H7 the antibodies draw in the bacteria, which stick to the silicon chip in a distinctive pattern. The pattern can be detected when a laser beam is passed over the chip.

In an article in the *Cornell News*, Carl Batt explains:

It is like a printing press. By stamping antibodies on the surface, the bacteria will be bound to the sensor and, they then form a pattern that can be read with a laser. It is a very fast, direct method for detecting bacteria. . . .

Bacterial contamination takes thousands of lives, sickens millions, and costs the health industry billions of dollars a year. If we had an early warning system, such as these biosensors could provide, we would be aware of the problem and able to attack it more efficiently.[59]

An Edible Vaccine

Another new development in biotechnology is the creation of an edible vaccine that protects people from food poisoning. Scientists theorize that genetically engineering plants to produce and contain tiny levels of proteins that are found on the surface of different pathogens can help humans develop immunity to those pathogens. The theory is based on the fact that contact with these proteins causes the immune system to attack. However, because only the protein and not the pathogen is present, food poisoning symptoms do not follow. Instead, the body produces antibodies in saliva that coat the surface of the digestive tract. These antibodies remain in the digestive tract where they can defend the body against future exposure to the pathogen.

Scientists have not yet been able to genetically engineer plants to manufacture the proteins found on food poisoning bacteria, but they have produced the protein from the hepatitis A virus in bananas, tomatoes, and potatoes. Laboratory tests on that protein have been so encouraging that clinical trials to determine the effectiveness of the vaccine are planned.

Vaccinating Animals

Other scientists are taking a different route. Rather than vaccinating humans against food poisoning pathogens, they are vaccinating animals. A vaccine that reduces *Salmonella* infection in poultry has already been developed. The vaccine is sprayed in the air or put in a bird's drinking water. However, because the vaccine reduces but does not eliminate *Salmonella* infection, scientists at the Southeast Poultry Research Laboratory in Athens, Georgia, are working on developing a more effective vaccine composed of dormant *Salmonella* pathogens. It differs from the

A farmworker sprays chicks with vaccine to reduce the likelihood that their meat will be contaminated by Salmonella.

older vaccine in that it is designed to permanently increase levels of *Salmonella* antibodies in a chicken's digestive tract. This decreases the chance that the pathogen can get a foothold in the animal's digestive tract and be shed in its feces. This is important because *Salmonella* shed in a bird's feces is the chief mode by which *Salmonella* spreads through a flock.

The vaccine is injected into chickens in two doses. Tests on its effectiveness have been promising. According to the study's director Peter Holt, "Reducing the prevalence of *S*. [*Salmonella*] *enteritidis* in poultry would likely cause a reduction in human infection from poultry and egg consumption. . . . We found that the new vaccine reduced *S. enteritidis* shedding 10 to 40 percent more effectively than the three commercial vaccines used by the U.S. poultry industry."[60]

Other scientists at the University of Georgia in Athens are trying to keep cows from shedding *E. coli* O157:H7 pathogens in their feces. To do this, scientists examined more than twelve hundred *E. coli* bacteria in cows' feces. Among these, they found eighteen strains of helpful *E. coli* that crowd out and kill *E. coli* O157:H7.

The scientists theorize that adding helpful *E. coli* to the feed of cows would raise the level of the helpful bacteria in the animals' digestive tracts. This would leave less room for *E. coli* O157:H7 in the cow's digestive tract, and eventually the helpful bacteria would crowd out and kill the *E. coli* O157:H7 pathogens. If the theory is correct, feeding cows a diet that includes helpful *E. coli* could be used as treatment for cows already harboring *E. coli* O157:H7. And starting calves on the helpful pathogen as soon as they are weaned would prevent *E. coli* O157:H7 from gaining a foothold in these animals' intestines. This would reduce the shedding of *E. coli* O157:H7 pathogens in cows' feces. The cumulative result would be more protection for the public.

To test the theory, in 2003 University of Georgia researchers measured, analyzed, and compared *E. coli* O157:H7 levels in two groups of calves' feces. One group was fed helpful *E. coli*, while the other group was not. The scientists found a significant reduction in *E. coli* O157:H7 in the treated calves' feces, but no reduction in the untreated calves. Next, in order to tell whether or not the helpful *E. coli* was crowding *E. coli* O157:H7 out of the calves' digestive tracts, the calves were slaughtered and their intestines were examined. The intestines of five out of six of the calves who were not fed helpful *E. coli* showed evidence of *E. coli* O157:H7, whereas the intestines of two out of six of the calves who were fed the helpful bacteria harbored the harmful bacteria. Researcher Michael Doyle explains: "Ultimately, we hope to not only use it as a treatment but also as a prophylactic [preventive], so by feeding it to calves, the bacteria won't be shed at all."[61]

Irradiated Food

Another step scientists have taken to prevent dangerous pathogens from infecting consumers is the development of food irradiation. Dubbed "cold pasteurization" by the food industry, food irradiation is a process in which food items such as meat, poultry, fish, fruit, vegetables, grains, and spices are exposed to radiation. The source of the radiation is either electron beams or gamma rays, both of which break chemical bonds in microorganisms. This destroys DNA in bacteria and parasites, making it impossible for these pathogens to reproduce. Once the pathogens can no longer multiply, they become inactive and die out. As with pasteurization, contamination of the irradiated food item is thus reduced or eliminated. And, just as an X-ray does not cause people to become radioactive, irradiated food does not become radioactive, nor does its taste or color change significantly.

In 2003 food science expert Carol Lorenzen of the University of Missouri in Columbia conducted research in which consumers were fed irradiated and nonirradiated beef, and their views on the color, taste, odor, and texture of the irradiated beef products were assessed. "With few exceptions," Lorenzen explains, "consumers found little difference in flavor or texture when comparing irradiated beef patties with non-irradiated beef patties."[62]

A number of other studies have been conducted in order to evaluate the effectiveness of irradiation. For example, a 2003 study conducted by the National Cattlemen's Beef Association took ground beef patties that were known to contain high levels of *E. coli* as well as *Salmonella* and *Listeria* and exposed the meat to electron beam irradiation. The meat was than analyzed, and the level of the pathogens was measured. According to research director James Kennedy, "This process reduced each of the three pathogens to a level that was undetectable and harmless to humans."[63]

Another 2003 test conducted by *Consumer Reports* measured pathogen levels in more than five hundred beef and chicken samples from sixty groceries throughout the United States before and after the meat was irradiated. The test found the irradiated beef and poultry had significantly lower bacteria levels than nonirradiated meat, but the irradiated meat still contained some bacteria. The researchers concluded that irradiation reduces but does not completely eliminate the risk of food poisoning. However, since irradiated meat contains fewer pathogens than nonirradiated meat, there is less chance that undercooked irradiated meat will cause food poisoning. Similarly, there are fewer pathogens in the drippings of irradiated meat, which reduces the chances of cross contamination.

This lab technician exposes a cylinder full of fruit to radiation that kills the DNA of any bacteria and parasites in the fruit.

Irradiation Is Controversial

Irradiated food items are available in forty countries throughout the world, including the United States where irradiated meat is sold in more than five thousand supermarkets. These include chains such as Pathmark, Super Value, Publix, and Food Emporium. It is also offered in restaurants such as Dairy Queen and Embers America.

Irradiated products are specially labeled with the radon symbol and words such as "treated with irradiation." This is to warn those consumers who, for a number of reasons, wish to avoid irradiated products.

In fact, irradiating food has caused some controversy. Some consumers fear the long-term effects of radiation on their bodies and point to the fact that there have not been any studies investigating the long-term health and side effects of frequent consumption by humans of irradiated food. There are also concerns that workers in irradiation plants may be exposed to dangerously high levels of radiation, and accidents could cause radioactive waste from irradiation plants to leak into the water supply. Because of these concerns, irradiated meat has not proven to be popular with American consumers.

As of spring 2004 irradiated beef sales accounted for only about 5 percent of all beef sales in the United States. Michael Jacobson,

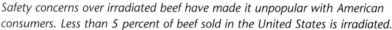

Safety concerns over irradiated beef have made it unpopular with American consumers. Less than 5 percent of beef sold in the United States is irradiated.

the executive director of the Center for Science in the Public Interest, an organization opposed to irradiation, explains: "While irradiation does kill bacteria, it involves the use of inherently dangerous materials and poses its own risks to workers, the environment and consumers."[64]

Despite these reservations, supporters of food irradiation say the benefits far outweigh the risks. Robert Tauxe, epidemiologist and chief of the Foodborne and Diarrheal Disease branch of the Centers for Disease Control in Atlanta, Georgia, estimates that if half of all beef, pork, and poultry produced in the United States were irradiated the results would be a 6 percent drop in all food poisoning cases reported in a given year. This translates to nine hundred thousand less food poisoning cases per year. Therefore, it is not surprising that irradiation has been endorsed by the World Health Organization, the UN Food and Agricultural Organization, the American Medical Association, the U.S. Department of Agriculture, and the Food and Drug Administration, among others.

Supporters of irradiated food say that current resistance to irradiated food is similar to that which occurred when pasteurization was introduced. At that time controversy also developed over the safety and benefits of pasteurizing milk. Irradiation supporters predict that as with pasteurization, resistance to irradiation will fade as consumers become more aware of the benefits.

Whether food irradiation will become widely accepted is still unclear. What is clear is that the work scientists are doing to keep dangerous pathogens from contaminating the food supply is having a positive effect. Indeed, the Centers for Disease Control report that the incidence of food poisoning from *E. coli* O157:H7 decreased 36 percent in 2004. With new developments in biotechnology and food irradiation, the prevalence of other pathogens is likely to decline as well. Food scientist and vice president of the Research and Knowledge Management branch of the National Cattlemen's Beef Association, James Reagan, explains: "While we still have a lot of work to do, it's promising to see and know we're moving in the right direction."[65]

Notes

Introduction: A Common Illness

1. Laura Day, "Food Travels from Farm to Fork," S.T.O.P., October 17, 2002. www.stop-usa.org/Policy_&_Outreach/Speeches/spch_laura_day.html.
2. Quoted in Morton Satin, *Food Alert!* New York: Checkmark, 1999, p. xi.
3. Brian Roe et al., "Consumer Research on Foodborne Illnesses," U.S. Food and Drug Administration Center for Food Safety and Applied Nutrition, www.cfsan.fda.gov/~lrd/abfoodb.html.
4. Nicols Fox, *Spoiled: Why Our Food Is Making Us Sick and What We Can Do About It.* New York: Penguin, 1997, pp. viii–ix.

Chapter 1: What Is Food Poisoning?

5. Bill Adler, "Bill Adler," S.T.O.P., 2002. www.stop-usa.org/Victim_Support/stories/adler_bill.html.
6. Quoted in Associated Press, "Unpasteurized Milk Has Its Fans", *Las Cruces Sun News*, April 4, 2004, p. 2A.
7. Quoted in Patrice Walsh, "Victims of Salmonella Poisoning Describe Their Pain," Marler Clark, August 15, 2002. www.marlerclark.com/news/brook-lea7.htm.
8. Quoted in Julie Vorman, "Most U.S. Beef Potentially Tainted with E. Coli," Reuters, Marler Clark, March 2, 2002. www.marlerclark.com/news/firm13.htm.
9. Fox, *Spoiled*, p. 216.
10. Satin, *Food Alert!*, p. 53.
11. Sue Doneth, "Regulatory Reform Testimony," S.T.O.P., February 24, 1998.www.safetables.org/Policy_&Outreach/Testimony/tt_reg_reform_02_1998.html.

12. Nicols Fox, *It Was Probably Something You Ate.* New York: Penguin, 1999, p. 7.

13. John, interview by author, Las Cruces, New Mexico, April 5, 2004.

14. Quoted in Fox, *Spoiled*, p. 194.

15. Mark, interview by author, Las Cruces, New Mexico, February 13, 2004.

16. Quoted in Fox, *Spoiled*, p. 263.

17. Marilyn, telephone interview by author, February 28, 2004.

Chapter 2: Diagnosis and Treatment

18. Bonnie, telephone interview by author, April 4, 2004.

19. Fox, *It Was Probably Something You Ate*, p. 166.

20. Darrylyn Blincoe, "Darrylyn Blincoe," S.T.O.P., 2001. www.stop-usa.org/Victim_Support/stories/blincoe_darrlyn.html.

21. John, interview by author.

22. Adler, "Bill Adler."

23. Quoted in Fox, *It Was Probably Something You Ate*, p. 35.

24. Fox, *It Was Probably Something You Ate*, p. 163.

25. John, interview.

26. Serena Gordon, "Serena Gordon," S.T.O.P., 2002. www.stop-usa.org/Victim_Support/stories/gordon_serena.html.

27. Gordon, "Serena Gordon."

28. Elton, interview by author, Las Cruces, New Mexico, April 14, 2004.

29. Laureen Spitz, "Zena Rose Spitz," S.T.O.P., August 1, 2000. www.stop-usa.org/Victim_Support/stories/spitz_zena.html.

Chapter 3: Avoiding Food Poisoning

30. Quoted in American Food Safety Institute, "Hidden Dangers at the Market," May 11, 2002. www.americanfoodsafety.com/news2.htm.

31. Satin, *Food Alert!* p. 79.

32. Cynthia J. Speegle, interview by author, April 17, 2004.

33. Day, "Food Travels From Farm To Fork."

34. Speegle, interview.

35. Speegle, interview.
36. Quoted in Jennifer Thomas, "Americans' Food Handling Habits Improving," HealthScout, September 27, 2002. www. healthscout.com/static/news/509326.html.
37. Fox, *It Was Probably Something You Ate*, p. 144.
38. Speegle, interview.
39. Elizabeth Scott and Paul Sockett, *How to Prevent Food Poisoning*. New York: John Wiley, 1998, p. 117.
40. Fox, *It Was Probably Something You Ate*, p. 141.
41. Quoted in Melanie Dabovich, "Salmonella Cases from Cantaloupe Prompt Warning," NMSU.edu. www.cahe.mnsu. edu/news/2001/070201_cantaloupe.html.
42. Satin, *Food Alert!*, p. 42.
43. Fox, *It Was Probably Something You Ate*, p. 128.
44. Speegle, interview.
45. Fox, *It Was Probably Something You Ate*, p. 134.
46. Quoted in Audrey Hingley, "Campylobacter: Low-Profile Bug Is Food Poisoning Leader," *FDA Consumer*, September/October 1999. www.cfsan.fda.gov/~dms/fdcampy. html.

Chapter 4: Protecting the Public

47. Quoted in ConsumerReports.org, "How Safe Is That Burger?" November 2002. www.consumerreports.org /main/ details2.jsp?CONTENT%3C%3Ecnt_id=163131&FOLDER %3C%3Efolder_id=18151.
48. Schild IGA.com, "Schild's Receives Five Star Rating," www. schildiga.com/htm/storenews/5star.htm.
49. Michael White, "Farmers and Ranchers", *Las Cruces Sun News*, January 17, 2004, p. 9A.
50. Marty, telephone interview by author, April 25, 2004.
51. Quoted in Associated Press, "Bush Orders Protection for Food Supply," MSNBC, February 3, 2004. www.msnbc.msn. com/id/4156537.
52. Quoted in Fredrick Golden, "What's Next?" *Time* Online Edition, November 5, 2001. www.time.com/time/magazine/ article/subscriber/0,10987,1101011105-181600,00.html.

53. Quoted in Associated Press, "Bush Orders Protection for Food Supply."

54. Quoted in Food Safety and Inspection Service, "Report: The USDA, Food Safety Mobile," January 2004. www.fsis.usda. gov/foodsafetymobile/2004report.htm.

55. Speegle, interview.

56. Quoted in Food Safety and Inspection Service, "Report."

Chapter 5: What the Future Holds

57. Satin, *Food Alert!* pp. 74–75.

58. Quoted in CNN.com, "Antibiotic Resistance a Growing Threat, WHO Reports," June 12, 2000. www.cnn.com/ 2000/HEALTH/06/12/antibiotic.resistance.

59. Quoted in David Brand, "Cornell Scientists Put Their 'Stamp' on a New Device to Seek Out Deadly Bacteria in Food or the Environment," *Cornell News*, April 7, 1998. www.news.cornell.edu/releases/April98/E-coli.bpf.html.

60. Quoted in Sharon Durham, "A Possible New Vaccine to KO Salmonella in Chicken Eggs," Food Safety Research Information Office USDA, May 2003. www.ars.usda.gov/is/ AR/archive/may03/eggs0503.pdf.

61. Quoted in Brandon Hancock, "Battling E. coli," Online Athens, June 22, 1998. www.onlineathens.com/1998/062298/ 0622.a11ecoli.html.

62. Quoted in Mary Jo Plutt, "Beef Irradiation Shown to Eliminate *E. coli* and Other Food-Borne Pathogens," National Cattlemen's Beef Association, www.Beef.org/dsp/dsp_location Contentcfm?locationId=106.

63. Quoted in Plutt, "Beef Irradiation Shown to Eliminate *E. coli* and Other Food-Borne Pathogens."

64. Quoted in Michael Fumento, "There's No Meat to Anti-Food Irradiation Claims," Fumento.com, www.Fumento.com.

65. Quoted in Michele Peterson and Sarah Sarosi, "Beef Industry Leaders Encouraged by Significant Reduction E. coli Incidence," National Cattlemen's Beef Association, April 30, 2004. www.beef.org/dsp/dsp_content.cfm?locationId=45& contentId=2610&contentTypeId=2.

Glossary

antacid: A medication that reduces stomach acid.

antidiarrheal medication: A medication that lessens the frequency of diarrhea episodes.

biotechnology: The use of living organisms to modify a plant or animal.

Campylobacter jejuni: A bacterium that is the most common cause of food poisoning.

Clostridium botulinum: A lethal bacteria that frequently develops in improperly canned foods.

digestive enzymes: Chemicals produced by the body, which help to break down food.

digestive tract: The pathway and organs in which food is broken down and absorbed by the body.

electrolytes: Substances found in the body that contain sodium and potassium and are essential for the body to function properly.

Electronic Foodborne Outbreak Reporting system: A national database in which information about food poisoning cases is recorded.

Escherichia coli (E. coli): A bacterium that frequently causes food poisoning.

esophagus: A tube that connects the mouth to the stomach.

Foodborne Disease Surveillance Network (FoodNet): An active surveillance network that tracks food poisoning cases.

Guillain-Barré Syndrome: A disorder that causes paralysis and is linked to food poisoning with *Campylobacter*.

Hazardous Analysis and Critical Control Points system (HACCP): A total quality control system that monitors food from the farm to the time it reaches the consumer.

hemolytic uremic syndrome (HUS): A complication of food poisoning that can cause kidney failure.

Lactobacillus: A genus of helpful bacteria found in yogurt.

Listeria monocytogenes: A bacterium that causes food poisoning and complications in pregnant women and fetuses.

pathogens: Disease-causing microorganisms.

plasmid transfer: A process in which a bacterium passes properties on to another species of bacteria.

PulseNet: A branch of FoodNet that uses DNA tests to link a food poisoning pathogen to its source.

Salmonella: A genus of bacteria that frequently cause food poisoning.

Organizations to Contact

Centers for Disease Control and Prevention (CDC)
1600 Clifton Rd. NE
Atlanta, GA 30333
(800) 311-3435
www.cdc.gov
Provides information on disease to the public. It also works to control and track disease outbreaks.

Safe Tables Our Priority (S.T.O.P.)
335 Court St., Suite 100
Brooklyn, NY 11231
(800) 350-STOP
www.stop-usa.org
Organized by food poisoning victims, this nonprofit organization provides information and support, and works to make the food supply safer.

U.S. Department of Agriculture, Food Safety and Inspection Service (FSIS)
1400 Independence Ave. SW
Washington, DC 20250
(202) 720-7943
www.usda.gov/agency/fsis/homepage.htm
Provides comprehensive information on all food safety issues. Offers numerous publications on food safety.

U.S. Food and Drug Administration, Center for Food Safety and Applied Nutrition
200 C St.
Washington, DC 20204
(800) FDA-4010
http://vm.cfsan.fda.gov/list.html
Provides information on food safety and pathogens. Offers the *Bad Bug Book*, a simple foodborne illness prevention and information pamphlet. Provides food safety advice to at-risk people.

For Further Reading

Books

William Dudley, ed., *Opposing Viewpoints: Epidemics.* San Diego: Greenhaven, 1999. The book is a collection of essays dealing with issues pertaining to epidemics, including a section on foodborne illness prevention.

Laura Egendorf, ed., *At Issue: Food Safety.* San Diego: Greenhaven, 2000. Fourteen essays with various views on food safety issues are presented in this book.

Sara Latta, *Food Poisoning and Foodborne Diseases.* Berkeley Heights, NJ: Enslow, 1999. Discusses the history, diagnosis, treatment, and prevention of foodborne diseases.

Web Sites

American Food Safety Institute (www.americanfoodsafety. com). Gives information about food safety, food safety news, and links to other related agencies.

ConsumerReports.org. (www.consumerreports.org). Provides an archive of articles describing tests on various consumer products including foods and restaurants.

Marler Clark (www.marlerclark.com). Marler Clark is a lawyer who represents victims of food poisoning. The Web site offers an archive of newspaper articles on food poisoning outbreaks.

National Cattlemen's Beef Association (www.beef.org). Provides information about the beef industry, steps the industry is taking to keep beef safe, and recent news about beef products.

National Food Safety Database (www.foodsafety.org). Gives a wealth of information on food safety issues and information on recent outbreaks.

National Food Safety Initiative (www.vm.cfsan.fda.gov~dms/fs toc.html). A clearinghouse for information on food safety.

USDA/FDA Foodborne Illness Education Information Center (www.na1.usda.gov/fnic/foodborne/foodborn.htm). Offers links to a number of publications and to related Web sites.

Works Consulted

Books

Nicols Fox, *It Was Probably Something You Ate.* New York: Penguin, 1999. The book examines dozens of pathogens and provides a guide to avoid infection.

———, *Spoiled: Why Our Food Is Making Us Sick and What We Can Do About It.* New York: Penguin, 1997. An investigative report that looks at different food poisoning outbreaks, what caused them, and food safety issues.

Morton Satin, *Food Alert!* New York: Checkmark, 1999. A comprehensive source on foodborne diseases. The book looks at different foods, the pathogens that infect them, and how people can protect themselves.

Elizabeth Scott and Paul Sockett, *How to Prevent Food Poisoning.* New York: John Wiley, 1998. Provides a concise guide on how to cook, eat, and handle food safely.

Periodicals

Associated Press, "Oyster Farmers, Dairy Ranchers Disagree over Pollution in Bay," *Las Cruces Sun News*, March 21, 2004.

———, "Unpasteurized Milk Has Its Fans," *Las Cruces Sun News*, April 4, 2004, p. 2A.

Michael White, "Farmers and Ranchers," *Las Cruces Sun News*, January 12, 2004.

Internet Sources

Bill Adler, "Bill Adler," S.T.O.P., 2002. www.stop-usa.org/ Victim_Support/stories/adler_bill.html.

American Food Safety Institute, "Hidden Dangers at the Market," May 11, 2002. www.americanfoodsafety.com/news2.htm.

Associated Press, "Bush Orders Protection for Food Supply," MSNBC, February 3, 2004. www.msnbc.msn.com/id/4156537.

Darrylyn Blincoe, "Darrylyn Blincoe," S.T.O.P., 2001.www. stop-usa.org/Victim_Support/stories/blincoe_darrylyn.html.

David Brand "Cornell Scientists Put Their 'Stamp' on a New Device to Seek Out Deadly Bacteria in Food or the Environment," Cornell News, April 7, 1998. www.news.cornell.edu/releases/April98/E-coli.bpf.html.

CNN.com, "Antibiotic Resistance a Growing Threat, WHO Reports," June 12, 2000. www.cnn.com/2000/HEALTH/06/12/antibiotic.resistance.

ConsumerReports.org, "How Safe Is That Burger?" November 2002. www.consumerreports.org/main/details2jsp?CONTENT%3C%3Ecnt_id=163131&FOLDER%3C%3Efolder_id=18151.

———,"Of Birds and Bacteria," January 2003. www.consumer reports.org/main/detailv2.jsp?CONTENT%3C%3Ecnt_id%20=297797.

Melanie Dabovich, "Salmonella Cases from Cantaloupe Prompt Warning," NMSU.edu. www.cahe.mnsu.edu/news/ 2001/070201_cantaloupe.htm.

Laura Day, "Food Travels from Farm to Fork," S.T.O.P., October 17, 2002. www.stop-usa.org/Policy_&_Outreach/Speeches/spch_laura_day.html.

Sue Doneth, "Regulatory Reform Testimony," S.T.O.P., February 24, 1998. www.safetables.org/Policy_&_Outreach/Testimony/tt_reg_reform_02_1998.html.

Sharon Durham, "A Possible New Vaccine to KO Salmonella in Chicken Eggs," Food Safety Research Information Office USDA, May 2003. www.ars.usda.gov/is/AR/archive/may03/eggs0503.pdf.

Food Safety and Inspection Service, "Report: The USDA, Food Safety Mobile," January 2004. www.fsis.usda.gov/foodsafety mobile/2004report.htm.

Michael Fumento, "There's No Meat to Anti-Food Irradiation Claims," Fumento.com, www.Fumento.com.

Fredrick Golden, "What's Next?" *Time* Online Edition, November 5, 2001. www.time.com/time/magazine/article/subscriber/0,10987,1101011105-181600,00.html.

Serena Gordon, "Serena Gordon," S.T.O.P., 2002. www.stop-usa.org/Victim_Support/stories/gordon_serena.html.

Brandon Hancock, "Battling E. coli," Online Athens, June 22, 1998. www.onlineathens.com/1998/062298/0622.a11ecoli.html.

Audrey Hingley, "Campylobacter: Low-Profile Bug Is Food Poisoning Leader," *FDA Consumer*, September-October 1999. www.cfsan.fda.gov/~dms/fdcampy.html.

Michele Peterson and Sarah Sarosi, "Beef Industry Leaders Encouraged by Significant Reduction in E. coli Incidence," National Cattlemen's Beef Association, April 30, 2004. www. beef.org/dsp/dsp_content.cfm?locationId=45&contentId=2610&content TypeId=2.

Mary Jo Plutt, "Beef Irradiation Shown to Eliminate *E. coli* and Other Food-Borne Pathogens," National Cattlemen's Beef Association, www.Beef.org/dsp/dsp_locationContentcfm?locationId=106.

Brian Roe et al., "Consumer Research on Foodborne Illnesses," U.S. Food and Drug Administration Center for Food Safety and Applied Nutrition, www.cfsan.fda.gov/~lrd/ab-foodb.html.

Schild IGA.com, "Schild's Receives Five Star Rating," www.schildiga.com/htm/storenews/5star.htm.

Laureen Spitz, "Zena Rose Spitz," S.T.O.P., August 1, 2000. www.stop-usa.org/Victim-Support/stories/spitz_zena.html.

Aparna Surendran, "Unsafe Meat Ended or Tragically Changed Their Lives," *Centre Daily Times*, June 4, 2003. www.centre daily.com/mld/centredaily/news/10864.htm.

Jennifer Thomas, "Americans' Food Handling Habits Improving," HealthScout, September 27, 2002. www.healthscout. com/static/news/509326.html.

USDA Food Safety and Inspection Service, "Food Safety and Security: What Consumers Need to Know," www.fsis.usda. gov/oa/topics/foodsec_cons.htm.

Julie Vorman, "Most U.S. Beef Potentially Tainted with E. Coli," Reuters, Marler Clark, March 2, 2002. www.marlerclark. com/news/firm13.htm.

Patrice Walsh, "Victims of Salmonella Poisoning Describe Their Pain," Marler Clark, August 15, 2002. www.marlerclark. com/news/brook-lea7.htm.

Index

Picture Credits

About the Author

Barbara Sheen has been a writer and educator for more than thirty years. She writes in English and Spanish. Her fiction and nonfiction have been published in the United States and Europe. She lives with her family in New Mexico. In her spare time she enjoys swimming, gardening, cooking, and reading.